Living Gospel Equality Now: Loving in the Heart of God

A Roman Catholic Woman Priest Story

by Bridget Mary Meehan, RCWP

"Living Gospel Equality Now: Loving in the Heart of God: A Roman Catholic Woman Priest Story," by Bridget Mary Meehan. ISBN 978-1-60264-696-4.

Published 2010 by Virtualbookworm.com Publishing Inc., P.O. Box 9949, College Station, TX 77842, US. ©2010, Bridget Mary Meehan. All rights reserved. No part of this publication may be reproduced, stored in a retrieval system, or transmitted in any form or by any means, electronic, mechanical, recording or otherwise, without the prior written permission of Bridget Mary Meehan.

Manufactured in the United States of America.

Dedication

This book is dedicated to Roman Catholic Women Priests globally and Mary Mother of Jesus Inclusive Catholic Community in Florida and in Northern Virginia, who are living the dream of Gospel equality as companions loving in the Heart of Love. In our inclusive communities, all are welcome at the Sacred Eucharistic Feast. We are walking on uncharted waters together as we offer the gift of a renewed priestly ministry in a people empowered community of equals.

Special thanks to my family for their loving support: my Dad, Jack, my brothers and sisters-in-laws Patrick and Valerie, Sean and Nancy, and my niece Katie and nephew Danny, my cousins, Margaret and Aidan Ryan, Noreen and Ger Davy, Mary and Bernie Ferns, Pat and Eileen Meehan, John and Mary D. Meehan, Seamus Meehan, Liz Murphy, Kate Donnelly, my aunts, Tess Murphy and Kathleen McNamara.

In this book, I fondly remember the women and men whose courage, wisdom and faith have reflected the love of God as sisters and friends: my mother, Bridie, my aunt, Molly, my spiritual sister, Regina Madonna Oliver, Irene Marshall, my friends Peg and Bob Bowen, Marcia Tibbitts, Geri Wayne, Jackie Burrows, Imogene and Mike Rigdon, Dick Fisher, Carol Ann and Lee Breyer, Jack and Helen Duffy, Sheila Carey, Margaret and Joe Mintern, Margaret Murray, Patricia O'Herlihy, Mairead O'Halloran, Megan Fitzgibbons, Dee Binda, Liz Smith, Sue Ritchey, Bernie Byrne, Rick and Ana Sapp, Judy Johnson, Sharon Friedman, and Paul Imsee. I am deeply grateful to Pastor Phil

Garrison, for his pastoral support of Mary Mother of Jesus Inclusive Catholic Community and to St. Andrew United Church of Christ Congregation who have shared their Sanctuary with us in Sarasota, Florida. I am thankful for all the members of Mary Mother of Jesus Inclusive Community and to the others in our growing communities who cannot be named here but who walk in solidarity with our movement for justice and equality in our church and world.

I owe a debt of gratitude to Judy Lee for her prophetic vision, helpful advice and editorial assistance in getting this manuscript ready for publication. I give thanks for the Association of Roman Catholic Women Priests: Eleonora Marinaro, Janice Sevre-Duszynska, Roberta Meehan, Dena O'Callaghan, Katy Zatsick, Mary Ellen Sheehan, Diane Dougherty, Miriam T. Picconi, Wanda Y. Russell, Joan. V. Throm, Judy Lee, Olga Alvarez and another candidate from South America, Morag Liebert, the first woman whom I ordained in Scotland, all our companions in the Roman Catholic Women Priests Movement and all our communities and supporters throughout the world. May you be forever blessed!

Table of Contents

Introduction.. i

Chapter One:
Memories of an Irish Childhood: The Catholic Church is in my DNA
.... 1

Chapter Two:
The Convent and Beyond...14

Chapter Three:
Reclaiming Our Ancient Heritage: Celebrating Liturgy in House
Churches 27

Chapter Four:
The Roman Catholic Women Priests Movement Grows...................37

Chapter Five:
Response to Excommunications: Outrage and Support of Women
Priests..47

Chapter Six:
There have always been Women Priests 59

Chapter Seven:
The Case for Women Priests: A Brief History and Overview 65

Chapter Eight:
Forever Loved, Forever Loving: The Essence of Theology for
Pastoral Care of One Another...78

Chapter Nine:
Experience Deep Love For God and For Others in the Heart of Love
....92

Chapter Ten:
Live Joyfully and Peacefully Each Day 100

Chapter Eleven:
Share Your Feelings With God..110

Chapter Twelve:
Wounded Healers: Celebrating Spiritual Empowerment............120

Chapter Thirteen:
Share With Soul Sisters 129

Chapter Fourteen:
Prayer Experiences for Loving from the Heart of God 138

Chapter Fifteen:
A Bishop's Prayer for the Church 141

AFTERWORD:
Celebrating Inclusive Liturgies 144

Introduction

My life has been full of surprises. From a young age, I had a sense of God's tender love drawing me, guiding me, and nurturing me. After our family rosary, I had little chats with God in front of the paintings of the Holy Family, the Blessed Mother, and the Sacred Heart. I don't remember the topics, but I sensed that the family of God in heaven was always on "stand-by," ready to help. This faith enabled me to survive the harsh discipline of the Irish school system. In chapter one, I disclose some of my earliest memories of the simple abundance our family shared when we lived in the small grey cottage overlooking the Erkina River in Coolkerry.

When I get comfortable, I usually encounter some event or experience that reveals something more, or urges me in a different direction, pushing me beyond my limits into new territory. I often argued with God about such abrupt changes but, usually, took the risk and went forward. And God has always provided *anam charas*, or "soul friends," to share faith and prayer. You will meet some of these courageous companions who have blessed my life with their loving support and wisdom. Remembering them still fills me with gratitude, sometimes tears, and often laughter.

Realizing my call to the priesthood and episcopate is the biggest surprise and challenge of all. This book weaves my story into the story of the Roman Catholic Women Priests. Interwoven as well is the spirituality and theology I live by, which is summed up in the phrase, "loving in the Heart of God." Jesus preached God's loving presence in the everyday experiences of caring for and serving neighbors. As Christians, we are called to be reflections of divine compassion and doers of justice in the here and now. *Living Gospel Equality Now - Loving in the Heart of God* gives the reader some thoughts on living a prayerful life that includes a deep commitment to equality and social justice for all of God's beloved people. At the end, there are some Liturgies that the reader may use and adapt.

At this time, I feel like I am walking on water, as I have been excommunicated from the official Roman Catholic Church. If I had a nickel for every "former" Catholic that I have met, who shared stories of alienation and marginalization, I'd be a wealthy woman. Surveys tell us that one out of ten adults in the United States is a former Catholic. If one excludes immigrants and converts, the Catholic Church in the U.S. has lost more than one-third of its members (http://anothervoice-greenleaf.org/). So now, in the Roman Catholic Women Priests Movement, it is a privilege to walk with many wounded brothers and sisters, offering the gift of hope and possibilities for a new Pentecost of spiritual renewal for the Catholic Church and beyond as we live Jesus' vision of passionate love for all in the Heart of God in inclusive grassroots communities.

Here we are on the edge of the church, leading the way, even if the Vatican is kicking and screaming! Who said it would be fun to be prophetic? Certainly not Miriam or Deborah in the Bible! But, like Miriam, Mary of Magdala, and our biblical foremothers, we are leading the way to a new way of living God's covenant in our church and world, one that is rooted in the Heart of God who leads us forward in our work for liberation, justice and equality. It is this promising new beginning that I share with you. This reality is what gets me up in the morning and fills my heart with joy. I live and breathe the emerging, empowered, spiritual community that is forming in many places and in my life within an enthusiastic community of believers who are living Gospel equality now.

We stand in solidarity with all those who are justice doers everywhere. No power on earth can shake our confidence that it is God's passionate love that makes us one. Here, we share a spiritual connection that will last forever. Here, we see in the eyes of another the image of God and experience human solidarity that moves us forward to proclaim the kindom now. I hope that this book may cast light on your own unique path. Come and see if God has some surprises in store for you!

Cottage, in Coolkerry, County Laois, Ireland, first Meehan family home in Ireland

The Meehan Family
Back Row, left to right: Nancy, Sean, Patrick, Bridget Mary, Dawn Vehmeier,
(friend) , Valerie
Front row, left to right: Jack , Danny holding dog Molly, Katie

Jack Meehan plays with Ballyroan Band on Aug 15, 2010 in Ballinkill, Ireland

Chapter One:
Memories of an Irish Childhood: The Catholic Church is in my DNA

I was born in Ireland in 1948 into a warm and loving Irish family. My mother, Bridie, liked to tell the story of my birth on my birthday each year. She recalled how the nuns took good care of her and of me. In those days, the fathers were not present at births that took place in hospitals. When my Dad arrived at the hospital, after cycling around 12 miles on his bike from Rathdowney to Abbeyleix, my mother proudly introduced their eight pound baby girl to him, saying, "Here she is now for you." We lived in a little gray cottage in Coolkerry, a rural area outside Rathdowney, where cows and sheep grazed in green fields across from the Erkina River. In this peaceful place, our family fished and played in its shallow, cool water. One of my favorite activities was taking an empty jam jar and plunging it into the river to catch pinkeens. We did not have many toys, but the earth was our playground. I molded and shaped mud pies in the rich moist soil of our garden. I imagined that my baked goods were culinary delights like my mother's rhubarb pies, scones, and cake bread! I loved to feel the wind blowing my hair as I walked through the fields dotted with daisies, buttercups, golden wildflowers, and purple heather. I played hide and seek in hay stacks with school chums and hunted for eggs that the hens laid in our bushes.

We had an open hearth and Mom always had a kettle on to boil, and every day we ate home-made soda bread that was simply delicious. The milk we drank came from our cow. My brother, Patrick, who was a year and one-half younger than me, and I walked home from school through the fields. We often stopped at Vester Campion's store on the way out of Rathdowney for "sweets" (penny candy or ice cream wafers) which I put on Dad's tab!

Sean, my youngest brother, was born in 1953. Dad worked at the bank as a porter and played in Billy Ryan's band on weekends. On Sundays, Dad took us for walks through the lovely countryside. As we strolled along leisurely, taking turns pushing Sean in the stroller, Dad told us enchanted stories of fairies, banshees, rabbits, and badgers. Each story introduced us to the mystical magic of the Celtic spirit and began the same way: "A long, long, long time ago in Ireland…"

My grandfather, Pat Beale, was a gentle, quiet man who often watched my brothers, Patrick and Sean, and me when we were small children. He took us out to pet Neddy, our donkey, and we watched as Mom milked the cow. Patrick and I had a pet lamb that we fed with a baby bottle. One time, the lamb swallowed the nipple from the bottle. We ran to tell Mom this tale of woe. She assured us that all would be well. The lamb did not get sick and we learned our lesson. Each day we drew water from a well near the river and used rain water to bathe. Our Saturday evening ritual included warm baths in large tubs placed on the kitchen floor. Dad and Mom worked as a team. One washed us and the other dried us, then off to bed. Even though we did not have central heat, just an open fire place and hot water bottles for our beds, I never remember being cold.

On Sundays, Grandfather yoked the pony to the trap and went to first Mass, then Mom and Dad went to second Mass. One time, when Grandfather was minding us, he fell asleep, and the three of us had a great time with the flour. When Mom and Dad came home, the flour was all over the floor. Later, they discovered that Grandfather was not feeling well. However, he gave exact instructions to my parents about "his last wishes." He told them that he was at peace, and that they were to treat everyone well at the wake and have lots of food and drink for all who came. He even told them that he wished to be buried in the

2

new cemetery near the town, not in Aghmacart where his wife was laid to rest. Then after a brief illness, Grandfather died and was laid out in a brown habit in his own bed. People came from miles around to his all-day and all-night "wake." Everyone remembered Pat by telling stories, laughing, crying, and toasting him as they enjoyed delicious food and drink. I still remember how peaceful he looked lying there on his bed. I spent the night of the wake and funeral day with neighbors. As the funeral procession passed, I counted the cars and thought that he must have been well-loved because such great crowds came to say farewell.

Our family was known as "the musical Meehans," and our home was always filled with the sound of music. Dad's father, Grandfather Jack Meehan, was one of the founding members of the Ballyroan Band in the late 1880s; his sons, my Dad, John (also called Jack), Jimmy, and Paddy, all played in this band. Dad was one of the youngest members of the band. I remember one night laying in my bed and hearing Dad play this beautiful melody on the trumpet, "O My Papa." He played three instruments: trumpet, saxophone, and trombone with many bands during his seventy-five year career, including playing with the Toby Bannon Family Band, Billy Ryan Band, the Jack Meehan band, and in the United States, the Foggy Bottom Five, the Hi-Fi's, and later, the Memory Aires. With gifted musicians, his band was popular in the Washington DC area from the 60's through the 90's. They played for Presidents, in embassies, country clubs, hotels, for weddings and anniversaries, and for Congressional events on Capitol Hill. In recent years, he plays both trumpet and saxophone for church gatherings and parties in Florida where we now live for half the year.

Ours has always been a praying family. In Ireland, we gathered in a circle around the turf fire each evening to recite the rosary. My mother was a firm believer in the saying, "a family that prays together stays together." She began every day and every event with the words, "In the name of God." I experienced at a young age that God was truly fond of me. I felt safe and secure in the circle of love of my family and my heavenly family. I enjoyed my chats with Jesus, Mary, the angels, and the saints. They were as real to me as my family. Perhaps the Irish prayer for protection best described my sense of God's presence: "The love and affection of the angels be to you. The love and affection of the saints be to you. The love and affection of heaven be to you, to guard you and cherish you" ("Blessings", *Carmina Gadelica*, Vol. 3, p. 207).

Neighbors often came by for cups of tea and homemade scones. Mom made delicious, mouth-watering scones slathered with fresh butter churned from the local farmer's creamery. The guests sat around the hearth fire and shared stories about local happenings such as births and deaths, sick cows, and foxes stealing hens. When John Dalton, the postal carrier, came by each day, Mom had a cup of tea ready for him, rain or shine. Hospitality, a hallmark of Celtic spirituality, was something I experienced everyday in our home. You never knew who was going to walk through our door, but my parents always gave them a warm welcome, Many times, Dad played the trumpet and saxophone, and the music and storytelling would last long into the night.

I attended senior infants and first class in the National School in Rathdowney. The Sisters of St. John of God taught there. I remember Sister Mary of the Angels slapping my hand with a ruler when I answered a question incorrectly. In Irish schools at that time, this was standard operating procedure. Often I had knots in my stomach for fear of being struck by the ruler. Obviously, school was not a fun place! Our only break was eating sandwiches and drinking hot tea at Pat Carroll's Pub at lunch time and playing marbles in the school yard during recess.

Early on, I was inspired by St. Brigit of Kildare, my patron saint. There were stories about her blend of Christian beliefs and pagan myths. St. Brigit was named after the Druidic mother goddess of fertility and abundance in ancient Ireland. St. Brigit saw to it that there was more than enough food, drink, and love to nourish all who came to her hearth and home. The story goes that one year there was not enough ale for seventeen of her churches. She changed water into beer to make sure that her churches were well-supplied for the season. On another occasion, she was given a basket of apples which she promptly gave away to the poor. When her benefactor complained, she said: "what is mine is theirs." No person who was poor or without resources ever left her presence without sustenance. Brigit even gave the feast day vestments of Bishop Conelth to the poor. In Trinity Church in Rathdowney where I celebrated my first communion, there is a beautiful stained glass window of St. Brigit dressed in purple and holding a pastoral staff. According to *The Irish Life of St. Brigit*, Bishop Mel ordained Brigit a bishop. According to the story, Bishop Mel, St. Patrick's nephew, who presided at the ceremony said: "Come, O holy Brigit, that a veil may be placed on your head before the other virgins." Then, filled with the grace of the Holy Spirit, the bishop read the form of ordaining a bishop over Brigit. While she was being consecrated, a brilliant fiery glow ascended from her head. MacCaille, Bishop Mel's assistant, complained that a bishop's rank was being bestowed upon a woman. Bishop Mel argued: "But I do not have any power in this matter. That dignity has been given by God to Brigit, beyond every other woman." Indeed, other bishops sat at the feet of Brigit's successor until the Synod of Kells ended the practice in 1152. St. Brigit was a woman of compassion, hospitality, and justice.

According to tradition, St. Brigit built her monastery in Kildare near a large Oak tree in 480 A.D. Both Brigit of Kildare and Hilda of Whitby founded monasteries in which women and men lived, some of whom lived a celibate life, while others were married couples with children, but all living as a Christian community, having dedicated their lives to Christ. In the sixth century, three Roman bishops sent a letter to two Breton priests, Lovocat and Cathern, banning women from presiding at Mass: "You celebrate the divine sacrifice of the Mass with the assistance of women... While you distribute the Eucharist, they take the chalice and administer the blood of Christ to the people... Renounce these abuses." My passion for justice and equality for women in the church is rooted in my Celtic soul that draws its inspiration from my patron saint, Brigit of Kildare.

Arriving and Settling in our new home in the U.S.A.

In June 1956, we emigrated to the United States. It took seven days to cross the stormy north Atlantic. One night, after Mom and Dad tucked us in our beds, they went up to the ballroom to attend a concert. I was the big sister in charge, so I locked the door and the three of us fell soundly asleep. We did not hear my parents calling our names nor their banging on the door, nor the steward sawing the door off its hinges to open it. That was the last time they left me in charge! Some other things I remember from our stormy journey are that we were all seasick, except for two-year old Sean who ran up and down the decks with my Dad chasing after him. As we sailed into New York Harbor, the majestic Statue of Liberty stood as a beacon of welcome to our new home. We were awestruck by the skyscrapers that loomed ahead of us and felt the heat of the sun beating down on us. We had heard that you could fry an egg on the sidewalks of New York; now we knew that it was probably true. Aunt Molly, mom's sister, Uncle Fergus, her husband, and Uncle Paddy, Mom's brother, warmly welcomed us. We spent our first night in a tiny apartment in a high rise building in New York City.

Then, the next day, we drove from New York to Philadelphia where cousins who had emigrated from Ireland decades before us lived. They prepared a wonderful feast for us. At their table, we tasted for the first time: ice tea, scrapple, and upside-down cake. After this grand meal, we drove to our new home in Arlington, Virginia. There, Aunt Molly presented me with a lovely doll that had a freckled face and long red braids.

We settled in quickly. Dad went to work in a maintenance job in the DC Public Schools and was invited to join a local band that played for the Irish Club in DC. Mom took care of Sean, prepared us for school, and babysat for a few young children in our home. Patrick started in 1st grade. After an evaluation, the principal decided that I could skip second grade, so I started in the third grade. I still remember my first year at Saint Thomas More School as a traumatic experience. I was a chubby little girl with curly hair. At recess, some of my classmates would tease me about the way I talked. Some called me "fatso" and would not let me join in their games. I often cried, couldn't concentrate in school, and felt as if I didn't belong. My schoolwork suffered as a result. To make matters worse, that year our nun became ill after the first month of school, and we had a number of substitute teachers who did not speak English.

Grade School in Virginia: Discovering the Power of Kindness and Affirmations

I did not begin to flourish in my new environment until the fourth grade, when a lovely, gentle nun, Sister Marita Louise, expressed her belief in me. She would stop by my desk and praise my efforts. I could tell from the sparkle in her eyes that she liked my Irish brogue. My spirit soared, my grades improved, and I made new friends. Affirmations always build us up.

Sometimes, we will not have a woman of grace like Sister Marita Louise shining God's light to heal our wounded spirit, and we will then need to do something ourselves to overcome the negative messages with positive affirmations that we repeat to ourselves or that others repeat to us.

Replacing

We can replace negative messages with positive, life-giving thoughts. Replacing: *You're not good enough!, You're not smart enough!, Don't even try that!, You're too young!, and You're too old!* with positive, life-giving messages such as: *I love and accept myself just the way I am!, I am a reflection of God's love!* and *I can do all things through God who strengthens me!* can completely transform our self-perceptions.

Speaking such truthful, gentle messages of love to ourselves as authors like Norman Vincent Peale in *The Power of Positive Thinking* recommend can nourish our spirits and open us to the Holy Spirit speaking in the depths of our souls.

When we repeat affirmations like these, we are hearing God speak to us, and we come to understand that God's love for us is beyond our imagination. Sometimes, "an angel" will appear in our lives, like Sr. Marita Louise, to encourage us. Sometimes, a book will guide us and sometimes divine providence will embrace us in some other way. Then, we will see ourselves as God sees us, and we will realize that our dreams for our life are only a shadow of God's dreams for us. Once we have known this kind of wondrous love, we will never be the same.

Growing up in the 50s 60s and attending Catholic elementary school was quite an experience. I was blessed with the friendship of Jackie Burrows, who was a year younger than me and lived in the neighborhood. We would get together to commiserate about how much homework we had in comparison to our public school neighbors, and of course, to compare notes on the nuns who taught us. Not all the nuns in the school were like Sr. Marita Louise. You could say that the nuns ruled, and, at times, used the ruler. They did not usually hit the girls, but the boys often got a crack of the ruler. Any major infraction of the rules cost the offender time in detention, which meant you had to stay after school and do some punishment, such as write 500 times, "I will not talk in class." One time, at recess, I had to stand at the blackboard and draw straight lines with a ruler. But, on the positive side, we learned respect and discipline. And, we got special holy days off from school, and this was a big plus! How we complained about the navy jumper and white blouses, our uniforms! I really disliked the blue beanie that we had to wear to church and the hours of homework we had to do each evening. However, we did learn to read and write! No question, the nuns were dedicated to our education and religious formation.

We spent hours practicing for the May procession each year, standing in straight rows in the parking lot as the sun bore down on our heads. As an eighth grade girl crowned Mary, we sang, "O Mary, we crown thee with blossoms today, queen of the angels, queen of the May." Even though I now cringe at the theology expressed in some of these Marian hymns, I must admit that they still touch my heart, bring back memories and remind me of Mary, as a reflection of God's nurturing love.

Before graduation, Sister Caritas, our young eighth grade teacher, took the girls in our class to visit the Immaculate Heart of Mary Motherhouse in Westchester, Pennsylvania. I remember being awed by the beauty of the chapel and the vibrant spirits of the novices who wore white veils. Our other two eighth grade nuns, God rest their souls, Sister Miriam John and Sister Miriam Clare, inspired fear in our hearts. They had no discipline problems. When we heard the clickers, we knew we better move or else! One click meant to stand up, two clicks meant to march single file into class. Three clicks, genuflect, and on it went. Ah, the joys of Catholic school days!

I attended Bishop Denis J. O'Connell High School. For the most part, I enjoyed the experience. There was a lot more freedom than in grade school. The only exception was Home Economics. Our first cooking project was making muffins. I don't know what I did, but they were the worst tasting concoctions that I ever put in my mouth. Sewing class was even worse. I basted and ripped out the hem of a skirt numerous times before getting it right and that was only with the patient help of my dear mother. Luckily for me, I aced the material in the book, but I was a disaster in the Lab! For me, High School was a time of serious study and reaching out and doing service projects in clubs, like putting on a party for children with special needs. I will never forget my high school friends, Sara Fahy, Peggy Mangum, and Clare Woodell. We shared our daily ups and downs and our crushes on cute boys as we rode to school in Clare's bright red car, often with the radio blasting music by the Beatles and other rock and roll artists of the 60s with the convertible roof pulled down. We thought we were really "cool." At that time, O'Connell High School was co-institutional—the girls were taught by the IHM nuns and the boys were taught by the Christian brothers. At that time, most of my friends smoked cigarettes. I took one puff and choked. That was my last puff! I remember the white dress that I wore to the senior prom and dancing with my date, John McNamara, to lively music. I think that music and laughter are the common language of the

Pilgrimages to our Homeland

Visiting or reminiscing about the places that have been significant in our lives is often helpful and affirming. Some people make a spiritual pilgrimage to the houses that have been home for them in the past. I made such a visit to the three-room cottage where I and my two brothers, Patrick and Sean, spent our earliest years together with our grandfather, Papa Beale. I walked to the spring where we drew water from the well; then, I went to Grogan to the church, now boarded up, where Mom and Dad were married fifty years ago. I sat in the church in Rathdowney where I made my first holy Communion, right under the stained-glass window of Saint Brigit. I stopped at Lady's Well, where Dad's band would play every year on the feast of the Assumption. We always carried home bottles of blessed water from Lady's Well. My last stop was the cemetery outside Ballyroan, to place my hand on the tombstone of Grandfather and Grandmother Meehan. These kinds of journeys affirm our very existence by putting us in touch with our roots. We stand on the shoulders of those who have gone before us. There is a thin veil between this world and the next, and all of life is laden with grace in our times of sorrow as in our times of joy. Our loved ones who have gone before us, who are now members of the communion of saints, stand ever ready to help us. They rest in the eternal embrace and are but a prayer away.

House Church (Early days 2007 left to right Jack Duffy, Dick Fisher, Jack Meehan (with saxophone), Bridget Mary Meehan, Helen Duffy

Chapter Two:
The Convent and Beyond

I frequently attended daily Mass in grade school and experienced there a special closeness to Christ in the Eucharist. The call to priesthood, I believe, was imbedded in my soul in those early years of my life, but I could not name it yet. So, I started the journey on the road set aside for women. After graduation from Bishop O'Connell High School, I entered the Congregation of the Sister Servants of the Immaculate Heart of Mary (IHM) at Villa Maria House of Studies in Immaculata, Pennsylvania. There were 90 postulants in my group, or "band," who entered the convent on the feast day of Our Lady of Sorrows, September 15, 1966. We were one of the last big bands. We may not have made the Blessed Mother weep, but we certainly tried the patience of our Postulant directors, Mother Elizabeth Ann Seton, Sister Sacre Coeur, and Sister James Dolores. The new motherhouse was still a work in progress, so there were workers all over the building. These men provided a major and, in some cases, a welcome distraction to the consternation of Mother Elizabeth Ann Seton, who tried to teach us custody of the eyes! In my case, that was a lost cause! We learned how to make tight beds that you could bounce a quarter on. I often found my bed stripped, which meant I had to remake it at lunch time. At our forty year reunion, a member of our band told us that Mother Seton once told her that when she did not know what to do with us, she sent us upstairs to brush our teeth. So, that is why we had so few cavities and trips to the dentist during our postulancy. Our rooms were separated by partitions and curtains. At night we were supposed to finish our day in sacred silence, which was an absolute ban on talking except in emergencies. A loud bell rang at 10:00 pm to signal the beginning of sacred silence, and another bell, usually after prayers in the morning, to signal its end. Our last act was to pray prostrate on the ground. Well, the first night, I prostrated the wrong way. I don't recall getting a diagram! I wondered what all the giggling was about during sacred silence! Another day, I was cleaning the toilets on the lower level of the motherhouse and accidentally swallowed a few drops of disinfectant that splashed up on my face. When the nun in charge, Sister Sacre Coeur, came to check on me, she just stood there and shook her head without saying a word. I guess she figured I'd live and one day I'd learn how to clean toilets!

I have so many wonderful memories of our band, the group I entered with forty-four years ago. In September 2006, we had our 40 year reunion at Stone Harbor, New Jersey for both the "ins" and "outs." What a nostalgic journey down memory lane! We told stories and laughed as we recalled those early days at Villa Maria Motherhouse. We also gave updates on our lives. I was heartened by the openness of the women to my priesthood. Even though some of the nuns disagreed with the path I am walking, they assured me of their prayers. Our band now keeps in touch through an internet listserve. We share requests for prayers and offer support on e-mail. It seems that the connections we made long ago have stood the test of time, and we remain a spiritual sisterhood. I am grateful for the ten years I spent as an IHM Sister. I learned a great deal about the spiritual life and about the gift of a consecrated life. Now, I know how to clean toilets, and that this too can be holy work!

Ten years after entering the convent, my mother had serious back surgery and I took a leave of absence. During that time, I met Sister Regina Madonna Oliver, also an Immaculate Heart of Mary Sister, who was on a leave of absence to care for her sick cousin. Regina and I joined a charismatic prayer group and became soul sisters as we shared our spiritual struggles to discover God's call in our lives. We both felt called to serve God in religious life but did not understand how we were going to continue to live this call outside our IHM congregation. I fussed and fumed with God to give me clear direction, but several years passed, and my only consolation was that Regina and I were on the same path, and we had a wise Trappist spiritual director who listened and affirmed that, painful as it was to hear, we were being called out of the familiar religious life community that we knew and loved, but our future remained a mystery. This meant that I had to give up the habit and ring. I still remember the sadness in my heart on the day that I walked up to St. Thomas More Convent and turned in these precious symbols of a life that I had lived for ten years. The next decade was a time for letting go and letting God— something that did not come naturally to an impatient woman like me. I often complained in my heart to heart conversations with God. My prayer was "lead me, guide me," but God was teaching me "trust" and patience. So, Regina and I investigated different religious orders, and even joined a diocesan community, Sisters for the Church. After years of prayer and discernment and testing the waters in this community, we met with some former IHMs who had joined Sisters for Christian Community. It was a huge "aha" moment. We had finally found the religious community whose vision we had carried in our hearts for years. The mission and vision of Sisters for Christian Community, a new paradigm of religious life, with several hundred Sisters, is "to birth a new understanding of the reign of God. We envision building a global community where all will be one, and where openness to the Spirit empowers us to live passionately the Gospel values of love, justice, reverence, forgiveness, nonviolence, equality, diversity, integrity and care for creation."

Finally, Regina and I made our commitment in the presence of kindred spirits, Sisters for Christian Community, and became members of the *Sophia* Region, a non-geographical region. Regina and I collaborated on retreats, workshops and co-authored several books: *Praying with a Passionate Heart, Affirmations from the Heart of God, A Promise of Presence, Praying with Celtic Holy Women* and *Heart Talks with Mother God*. It was a great joy for both of us that Regina, although in ill health, was able to travel to Pittsburgh and present me for priestly ordination. I was also blessed by the presence of three other women from Sisters for Christian Community: Consilia Karli, Carla Barr, and Rosa Gamarra. After a major illness, Sister Regina died in 2007. I miss her very much, but feel that she continues to pray for me, for our religious community, and for the Roman Catholic Women Priests' Movement. As Sisters for Christian Community, our vision continues to evolve. Today, as an empowered community of women religious, we are challenged to image God in our midst in light of our new understanding of the mystical oneness we share, connecting all life in the cosmos.

Pastoral Ministry Experience

Through the years, I became aware that other denominations were ordaining women, and I pledged myself to work for ordination of women in the Roman Catholic Church. I strongly sensed God's call to priesthood when I worked for fifteen years as a pastoral associate at Ft. Myer Chapel in Arlington, Virginia. Divine Providence played a major role in opening up a pastoral ministry position there. It is another one of those amazing grace stories!

On May 17, 1980, I graduated from Catholic University with an M.A. degree in religious studies. At that time, I wondered where God would lead me next. I didn't see any openings in pastoral ministry in the diocese of Arlington, and I didn't want to move out of the area.

Several weeks after graduation, Irene Marshall, a friend who transported Mom and Aunt Molly to Mass each day, invited me to join them. So, one day I rode with them to Ft. Myer Chapel. After the liturgy, Chaplain John Weyand greeted me and, after finding out my background, he asked if I had any ideas on spiritual renewal for parish communities. I offered to work with a team and present a Life in the Spirit Seminar. So, Fr. John invited some parishioners to join us on a team: Irene Marshall, Tom Goddard, Donna Mogan, and Kay Graf. After the six week seminar, we started the Bread of Life prayer group which met on Wednesday evenings. We gathered in a comfortable lounge in the basement of the Post Chapel. Seated in a circle, we began our prayer time with praise music, the liturgy of the Word, a shared homily, and intercessory prayer. Then, we moved upstairs into the Blessed Sacrament Chapel to continue our celebration with the Liturgy of the Eucharist. Afterwards, we had prayer rooms where individuals came for prayer with one of our ministry teams.

After a few months, the senior Catholic Chaplain, Warren Tierney, invited me for an interview. At that time he affirmed my ministry, and asked if I'd be interested in pastoral ministry at Ft. Myer Chapel. I said "yes." He then directed me to write the job description of a pastoral associate that I thought would serve this community. After I turned it in, Chaplain Tierney submitted it to the officials. Several months later, it was approved, and I was hired. What a surprise; where God was leading me had been right in front of me, close to home, and my dream ministry, too! My prayers were answered, and now I was moving out of my comfort zone into a new pastoral ministry setting, different from teaching school as an Immaculate Heart of Mary Sister!

I learned a lot about ministry from the chaplains with whom I worked in an interfaith facility. The chaplains modeled team ministry and shared a common worship space. A major part of my job was to provide leadership training for adult ministers in the Catholic community. I invited couples who were interested in sharing their experiences with engaged couples to become part of a couple sponsor team, parents to share their faith with new parents in a baptismal team ministry, and retirees to visit the sick and homebound in a CROSS/Christians Reach Out to Serve the Sick and Suffering Ministry. I initiated the Rite of Christian Initiation for Adults program and the family intergenerational religious education program. I recommended that we build unity and community in our chapel community by scheduling an annual Ecumenical Retreat for Protestant and Catholic Congregations. The chaplains liked this idea. So, we invited Peg Bowen, a talented and energetic organizer from the Catholic Community, to plan and coordinate this spiritual weekend. If the retreat leader was

Catholic one year, the following year, the retreat leader was Protestant. I am happy to report that Ft. Myer Chapel still has an annual Ecumenical Retreat, and that Peg and her husband Bob Bowen still serve in ministry in this faith community.

I will be forever grateful to Chaplain Frank Keefe, a priest, who became a wise mentor. He officiated at second marriages of elderly couples who could not get annulments. Afterwards, he'd say to me: "Sister, I am acting according to my conscience." Our Midnight Masses were packed with families and visitors. Each year, before this festive liturgy, Fr. Keefe looked at me with a big grin and said: "Sister, tonight, I am giving the people the greatest gift of all, general absolution. I cannot possibly hear all those confessions!" Even though Fr. Keefe died several years ago, his memory lives on my heart. He taught me that good "pastoring" is a work of the heart. It is about serving God's people, loving in the heart of God. Obeying church rules is always secondary to obeying one's conscience. If we ask ourselves" what would Jesus do?" in a situation and do it, we will be on the right track. Chaplain Keefe and his buddy, Chaplain Joe Mulqueen, often came by our home for tea and scones. Both priests were mentors and became friends of mine and of our family.

In the army there was a shortage of priests, so I was asked to do everything except preside at Mass and sacraments. Often when I conducted a communion service in the absence of a Catholic priest, the people expressed their gratitude for the "lovely Mass." Even though I made it clear that this was a Communion Service, they often called it a Mass. So, it dawned on me that they'd easily accept me as their priest if I was ordained. Often I prepared couples for marriage with the assistance of a couple functioning as a ministry team, but the chaplain, who did not even know the couple, officiated at their wedding. Some of the chaplains that I worked with would have been delighted if I could have officiated at weddings and anointed the sick. They had so many duties with the military that most of these chaplains would have gladly shared the ministry with me. So, my call to priestly ministry over the years was gradually confirmed by this close-knit community, and by several communities that I served over the past twelve years.

One of these communities in Northern Virginia, called " The Gathering" came from a program of renewal that began in our local parish. In 1995, Fr. Tuck Grinnell, the pastor of St. Anthony's Parish, asked me to lead one of these home-based groups. So, about a dozen parishioners met monthly for twelve years to reflect on the Sunday Scripture readings in my home in preparation for liturgy. Most of the members were elderly. My mother, Bridie, and aunt, Molly, participated in this group for a few years before they died. It felt like our family had come full circle from the early days of family prayer in Ireland and in the U.S. in our home to an extended family , praying and sharing, in our home. Lots of times, the group had debates on the future direction of the church, but we grew closer, not further apart, because of our mutual respect for one another. The "Gathering" developed an intercessory prayer ministry for the larger community. We kept a list of prayer requests that we prayed for each day and that we prayed for when we met as a community. Since Dad and I live in Florida for half of the year, and several members of the group have died, the community no longer meets on a regular basis. However, we do keep in touch and get together for special occasions. Marcia Tibbitts, a community member and friend, shares her gifts of compassionate caregiving with Dad and me. When I am out of town at ordinations or meetings, Marcia gives Dad insulin shots and checks his blood pressure. I know that he is in good hands with Nurse Marcia. Marcia also has designed three brightly-colored scrapbooks with photos and articles about my RCWP ministry.

In 2005, I was invited by a group of women from different faith traditions to lead discussions on women of the Bible. During one of these sessions, I shared that Judy Johnson, a friend, had invited me to attend the first ordinations of women priests in North America. The ceremony was scheduled to take place on a boat sailing on the St. Lawrence Seaway. The women were delighted and told me that not only should I attend, but that I should be ordained and that they wanted me to be their priest! One woman even donated her frequent flyer miles so I could fly free to Canada. The next day, I picked up a tube of suntan lotion that said, "get on the boat." I laughed and thanked God for yet another sign! So as they say, "the rest is history!"

As I stood in a long line to embark on the boat on July 25, 2005 in Gananoque, Canada, I remember the heat, the crowds of people, and the media presence everywhere. Bishop Gisela Forster from Germany, one of the women who was ordained on the Danube, greeted me and said that she thought that I should be ordained. I felt that her comment was another of those positive signs from Divine Providence that sometimes happen when you are meant to do something. As the women lay prostrate on the floor of the boat symbolizing the offering of their lives in servant priesthood, the assembly sang the Litany of the Saints, I could feel the gentle rocking of the boat and hear the splash of the waves as we sailed down the scenic St. Lawrence Seaway that borders Canada and the United States. The nine newly ordained women were "rocking" the institutional church by their prophetic obedience to the Spirit. I sensed that nothing would ever be the same once we had Roman Catholic Women Priests in North America. It was a seismic shift!

Soon after I returned from Canada, I applied and was accepted as a candidate. I already had the educational and pastoral experience background. In 1987, I had been the first woman and first Roman Catholic to receive a Doctor of Ministry from Virginia Episcopal Seminary in Alexandria, Virginia. I completed the preparation program which consisted of ten units of sacramental and pastoral theology under the mentorship of Bishop Patricia Fresen. On July 31, 2006, I was one of the twelve women ordained by three women bishops, Patricia Fresen, Gisela Forster, and Ida Raming, aboard the Riverboat Majestic, sailing down the three Pittsburgh Rivers. My Dad, brother, Patrick, Sister in Christ, Regina Madonna Oliver, and close friends, Peg and Bob Bowen, Marcia Tibbitts, Dawn Vehmeier, Mary Fitzgibbons, Dee Binda, Rick and Ana Sapp, Geri Wayne, Kay Graf, Donna Mogan, Liz Smith, Sue Ritchey and Sharon and Paul Imsee attended. My sister-in-law, Nancy, who worked for a Catholic School, was told that she could risk her job if she attended. Nancy decided, with the support of our family, that it

fledging community sang and opened their hearts to one another as they shared stories of their faith lives during the shared homily and recited the Eucharistic Prayers together. "Do this in memory of me," we prayed, and so we took Jesus' words literally as we celebrated together the mysteries of our faith at the sacred banquet.

As devout Roman Catholics have done through the ages in their local churches, we, the Body of Christ, are sharing the Eucharist, the Body of Christ, with the Body of Christ. We, the gathered assembly, celebrate our mystical oneness with Christ with all the saints who have gone before us and with the pilgrim people of God, the entire church. The only difference is that I am a Roman Catholic woman priest presiding in a church that has yet to accept women's ordination in our time, even though women served the Christian community in ordained ministry during its first twelve hundred years. (The reader might see Gary Macy, *The Hidden History of Women's Ordination*, and Ute Eisen, *Women Officeholders in Early Christianity: Epigraphical and Literary Studies*.)

Our energized community is not waiting for permission from church authorities. As one woman noted, "the Vatican will catch up one of these days." Until then, we say: "let's praise God, you holy people with holy music." And so we did, every week in the winter in our cozy home only a few miles from the Gulf of Mexico from 2006-2008.

Barbara, from Peoria, Illinois, called me a few years ago to find out if we had women priests in Peoria. There is something that connects on a deep level with people as they experience women presiding at Eucharist, and as they co-celebrate Eucharist. We have received regular requests from people across the country who are looking for women priests' communities.

Christ the Servant Community

Some are even calling forth individuals to be ordained by RCWP and asking them to continue their ministries in the local community. This is the situation with Christ the Servant Community in Ontario, Canada. In 2005, after the first ordinations in North America, Rev. Ed Cachia spoke publicly in favor of women's ordination and in support of the St. Lawrence RCWP ordinations in 2005. As a result, he was removed from his parish and disciplined by his bishop. Christ the Servant Community formed in support of him. After a period of prayer and discernment, Rev. Ed sought reconciliation with the Church, but church officials did not restore him to active parish ministry. Later, Fr. Ed married. But, the community he nourished at Christ the Servant had become empowered. They began a dialogue with RCWP/Canada in the Fall of 2006. In 2007, they invited Marie Bouclin, after she was ordained a Roman Catholic Woman priest, and Kevin Fitzgerald, a priest in the Old Catholic Church, to serve their community. Now, one of their community members, Gary O'Dwyer, who has been ordained by Abba Ministries, serves as their pastor. A woman from this community now has been called to servant priesthood. She has completed her theological studies and is now a candidate in the Roman Catholic Women Priests Movement. Christ the Servant community is leading the way toward a people empowered, justice-seeking church. This path could be a viable option for many other Catholic communities who love their faith and want to stay together as a community. The people of God are the church. So, when a diocese decides that a parish must close, Catholic communities could follow Christ the Servant's example and call forth their own pastoral leadership.

Priest Partner Couples Stand around altar with Congregation: right to left : Imogene and Michael Rigdon, Bridget Mary Meehan, Lee Breyer at St. Andrew United Church of Christ, Sarasota, Florida during Saturday evening liturgy for Mary Mother of Jesus Inclusive Catholic Community

Bridget Mary Meehan, Priest Partner Couple Lee and Carol Ann Breyer at St. Andrew United Church of Christ, Sarasota, Florida at Mary Mother of Jesus Inclusive Catholic Community liturgy

Chapter Three:
Reclaiming Our Ancient Heritage: Celebrating Liturgy in House Churches

There are millions of Catholics, according to surveys, who have left the church for one reason or another. It is our hope to offer them a warm welcome home! Since I am Irish by birth, offering hospitality is part of my cultural inheritance. We are people-friendly. Our liturgies are festive, full of song, music, clapping, singing, and even swaying now and again! One woman, Marie, who had been divorced and remarried, cried when she received communion at our house church. After a hostile encounter with a priest years ago, she felt unworthy to receive the Eucharist in her parish community. Now she said: "I feel like I have come home at last." Marie has invited me to celebrate Mass in her home in Florida. I plan to do "home Masses" when people ask. When people are sick and infirm, I gather with their family and friends in their own surroundings to administer the sacrament of the anointing of the sick in a communal setting, inviting others to also anoint and pray together for healing and wholeness.

In 21st century Catholic worship, centered in the Eucharistic thanks-giving and self-giving of Jesus, is once again being celebrated in house churches. Roman Catholic Women Priests are leading the way to reclaim the ancient tradition of Eucharistic table sharing that builds community. Like the holy women and men of the early church, we are gathering together to break open our lives, to share bread and wine in memory of Jesus, and to live the Christ-Presence in our work for justice, peace and equality in our world.

Therefore, it is appropriate that the community, not the priest alone, say the words of consecration together. Gary Macy, chairperson of the Theology and Religious Studies Department at the University of San Diego, concludes that in the understanding of the medieval mind, regardless of who spoke the words of consecration—man or woman, ordained or community—the Christ presence became a reality in the midst of the assembly.

Mary Mother of Jesus Inclusive Catholic Community House Church: 2006-2007

Recalling his first impression of our house church, Dick Fisher wrote, "This "holy ground" is warmly welcoming. Here a loving, caring God is made better known. Saturday evening mass is a joyful experience. The stress of being led by self-appointed clergy of a too often false certitude, has disappeared entirely."

Dr. Judith Lee, who later became a Roman Catholic Woman priest with a powerful ministry to the poor and homeless in the Ft. Myers area, came to one of our liturgies in Sarasota in 2007. She summed up the vision of contemporary house churches in the ministry of the Catholic faithful: "It is a community of equals before God, empowered to go out and be the arms and hands of Christ in the world. Let the people say Amen! They already have!"

Helen Duffy, a member of our house church, said that she had bad dreams that the papal nuncio would come through our doors, and this would not be a good thing! Her husband, Jack, has reminded us on numerous occasions that he has had it with our Our Lady of Perpetual Responsibility and Guilt and he is delighted to praise God at Mary, Mother of Jesus. He does not share his wife's concern with the punitive arm of the hierarchy!

This hopefulness became evident when a group of our Irish friends (who normally pay, pray, and obey in their local parishes each week) invited me to bless a new home and celebrate a Sunday liturgy there. Using holy water from Mary's Shrine in Knock, Ireland, all of us walked throughout the house, blessing each room as we processed. Usually, our Irish friends do not volunteer to read in church. Yet, they felt comfortable in house church and read, shared in the dialogue homily, and prayed the words of consecration together with me. When all was finished, they pronounced the liturgy "brilliant!" They noted that it was a big step forward from their worship experience at Sunday liturgy in the local parish, and one in which Ireland's patron saint, Brigit, Bishop of Kildare, would have felt right at home — blessing everything with water to remind us of God's protective presence! (St. Brigit's cross hangs over the door of many Irish homes and barns as a sign of protection and blessing).

Roman Catholic Women Priests are dreaming daring dreams and discovering fresh visions. Jack Duffy shared what it means to worship in spirit and truth as the Body of Christ: "In this small, intimate, friendly, around-the-table setting, the worship was deep, spiritual, holy. We could all really sense that Jesus was there with us. The Masses celebrated by Bridget Mary, a validly ordained Roman Catholic priest, were no different from those we have attended done by other validly ordained male priests. Her ordination was completely valid; as are the Masses at which she officiates. Having a woman priest may seem 'new' and radical; however, it is fairly certain that women—and married men—had been the ones presiding at the Eucharistic celebrations in the early Christian Church. So when the Roman Catholic Church finally evolves to this 'new' and radical way of operating, it isn't really new at all. A prominent US Catholic Bishop from Detroit speaking here in Sarasota two weeks ago predicted the Church of the future will most likely see married and female priests."

Yes, indeed, we have come full circle. Like our sisters and brothers in the early Christian community, we believe that Christ is calling us to go forth, filled with God's love and compassion, to minister as partners and equals with all of God's people. The world is our parish and, as my Southern neighbors say, y'all come! And, so the people came.

Mary Mother of Jesus Inclusive Catholic Community Grows 2008-2010

In 2008, Mary Mother of Jesus Catholic Community decided to run an ad in the local *Sarasota Herald Tribune,* inviting all to attend an inclusive Catholic Mass weekly in our house church, which still at this point met in my home. The Roman Catholic Diocese of Venice responded immediately. They asked the *Herald-Tribune* to stop running this religious service announcement, but the editors decided not to comply. Then the diocese placed an announcement in the *Herald-Tribune* stating that "no such worship site exists within the Diocese, nor is it recognized by the Diocese of Venice" (see article "Religious Fraud or Religious Conviction," by Tom Lyons, *Sarasota Herald Tribune*, Feb.26, 2008).

It was the "snowbird season" when people came to Florida to enjoy the sunshine and escape the cold weather. After the bishop's disapproval, I received lots of phone calls and each week more people crowded into my tiny living room for Mass. On several occasions, we had to borrow our neighbor's chairs. Then parking became a problem because there were too many cars on our street and the Homeowners' Association asked that we park in a lot about a half-mile away, which meant volunteers had to do traffic control and shuttle people back and forth from the parking lot to our mobile home. We continued to place our ad in the newspaper.

After several letters of protest from our community were published in the newspaper, ABC TV showed up and filmed a Mass in our home. They interviewed Jack Duffy, a member of our community, who said: "A church like Epiphany Cathedral is so big and huge but this is more personal, more intimate and we can feel a little more tighter relationship with Jesus....I can see where officials in the Catholic church might not approve of it but as my wife so clearly says, we are spirit filled common sense Catholics. This just makes sense." Jack, in a letter to the editor, pointed out that while it was true that we were not in the Venice Diocese, we did celebrate an authentic Mass each week.

The ABC interview quoted my conviction that our Roman Catholic Women Priests' initiative was grounded in Gospel equality and in early church history: "Jesus was a rule breaker and he got in plenty of trouble for breaking the rules." Many people do not know that women were ordained for the first 1200 years of Christianity.

Adela Gonzales White, a spokesperson for the Diocese of Venice stated: "Bridget Mary Meehan and her house church are not associated with the Catholic Diocese of Venice" ("Sarasota woman says she's a Catholic priest" ABC/Suncoast, March 5, 2008).

After this program aired, the Venice Diocese took out ads listing Sunday Liturgies. I was surprised they did not list the Saturday evening liturgies since Mary Mother of Jesus Catholic Community celebrated Mass on Sat evenings. Did this mean that they were ceding Saturday evening liturgies to Mary Mother of Jesus Inclusive Catholic Community?

Regardless of their intent, our community tripled in size. As a result, we needed to move our Saturday evening liturgies from my home to a larger home. After three weeks, we outgrew the larger home and found a beautiful sacred space at St. Andrew United Church of Christ. Pastor Phil Garrison and his congregation offered a warm welcome to our fledging community. There, we hold our Saturday evening liturgies at 6:00 PM. All are welcome to receive Eucharist at the banquet of Christ's love at Mary Mother of Jesus Catholic Community.

It appears that every time the hierarchy censures Roman Catholic Women Priests and condemns our inclusive worshipping communities, we grow. Sometimes, when incidents like the one above happen, I wonder if we should send a "thank you" note to the bishop. I don't think the hierarchy gets it; the more they denounce us, the more we are blessed, often in ways beyond our wildest dreams.

Our community now has a leadership circle that consists of two married priest couples: Mike and Imogene Rigdon and Lee and Carol Ann Breyer; Sheila Carey, a liturgical dancer; Jack Meehan, our music minister; Dick Fisher; Jack and Helen Duffy; and others who cannot be named because of the role they play in the institutional church. We gather to set policy and make decisions. Our leadership circle is open to members of our community who are invited to share their gifts as we grow in loving service to the people of God in the Sarasota area.

Leadership Circle of Mary Mother of Jesus Inclusive Catholic Community Speaks Out

Sheila Carey: "HOME"
Sheila Carey says: "When I think of our Mary Mother of Jesus Community (MMOJ) I think of HOME—for this is what it has

become for me. For a long time, I had been floundering in a Catholic church from which I was feeling increasingly alienated. My heart and my soul were seeking a true home, and I found that the very first time I walked into Bridget Mary's home in 2008, where at that time she was holding Mass every Saturday evening. She stood at her front door, full of life and welcoming—and embraced me warmly. Her small congregation were also most cordial and hospitable; I believe hospitality is a very important spiritual gift--and MMOJ is overflowing with this! Bridget Mary is following her calling from God to ministry---she takes this very seriously and, at the same time, is witty and lighthearted. When my mother lay dying in Venice Hospital, I called Bridget Mary to anoint her; she came down from Sarasota immediately. The hospital's Catholic chaplain walked into Mom's room just after Bridget Mary had anointed her. He, not knowing this, anointed her also! And when I, a nurse who anoints my patients, arrived—I also anointed Mom! So within an hour, she had 3 anointings--we call it the "triple crown!" Another way MMOJ has powerfully affected my life: since 1977 I have been a Liturgical dancer in various places I have lived--and joyfully participated in many a celebration of life--and death (i.e., my father's funeral Mass). I had been prevented from dancing at Mass in my former parish, Epiphany Cathedral in Venice—due to Bishop Dewane's negative attitude towards this gift. I had no such rejection from MMOJ folks-- all of them have been incredibly encouraging, and I've shared the gift of Sacred Dance with them on many occasions—one of the highlights was last Feb. 6th when Bridget Mary ordained two new women priests. The joy was contagious as I danced the whole group into the church (St. Andrew's in Sarasota) for the Processional, and we danced out as well for the Recessional! Being involved in MMOJ has caused me to grow as a person in all ways—spiritually, emotionally, mentally, even physically—I am the healthiest and happiest I have been in years. Thank you, Bridget Mary and MMOJ!!"

Carol Ann and Lee Breyer:
Carol Ann and Lee Breyer, a married priest couple who live in Bradenton, Florida, participate in the Leadership Circle. Lee is a priest partner and Carol Ann is a minister of the Eucharist and

liturgist. Both help plan our liturgies. Here, they share their reflections on Mary Mother of Jesus Inclusive Catholic Community.

Lee Breyer, Priest Partner: "From Superiority To Equality"

"As someone who spent almost two decades in exclusively male schools, namely, a traditional Catholic seminary, I was accustomed to living in a single gender society with single gender orientation. While I was uncomfortable with it (graduate education in a coed environment will do that to you), the requirements of a patriarchal church limited public behavior that differed from the male norm.

Forty plus years of working with men and women in "underground home liturgies" involved acknowledging and welcoming the participation of everyone engaged in every part of the liturgy. There was no place for masculine domination or single "performances." That was a lesson learned for life and worship.

Quite naturally, this led to Mary, Mother of Jesus, Catholic Community where there is no clerical distinction among those participating in the liturgy. All are equals; all are involved in every part of the service; all worship together, create the miracle of the Eucharist, and bless one another. As Paul wrote to the church communities in the region of Galatia: "In Christ, there is no... male or female, for you are all one in Christ Jesus" (Galatians 3: 28 in *The Inclusive New Testament*, Priests for Equality).

MMOJ, without rancor toward any other organization, is creating a new form of church community for those people whose search brings them to its "tent."

Theologian Sandra Schneiders described the critical necessity of developing such equalitarian communities. According to her, "equal rights for women in the church is crucially important, but the radical dismantling of patriarchy, one of whose pernicious manifestations is the oppression of women, is essential, not only to the life of the church, but for the future of the human race" ("God is the Question and God is the Answer" in *Spiritual Questions for the Twenty-First Century*, Orbis Books).

Carol Ann Breyer: "We Celebrate, We Believe"

"In their flight from patriarchy, zealous women need to guard against the temptation to "get even." After years of being lay subjects in a sexist Church, it is only natural to react with a

life of a "cafeteria Catholic." My spirit was yearning for spiritual direction and a community of believers who were not beholden to patriarchal authority. At last my husband and I found it in Bridget Mary Meehan's house church, Mary Mother of Jesus. It is an inclusive community. All are welcome—gays, sinners, all people seeking the meaning of life, married priests, and even their wives . Each of us is still always loved by Jesus. We are constantly reminded that we are all the hearts and hands of Jesus in the world today. How wonderful!

And so my married priest husband, Michael and I began to celebrate the life of Jesus together in very spiritual and accepting community. Thank you, God, for this gift!"

Program Coordinator Eleonora Marinaro presents Dena O'Callaghan and Katy Zatsick for ordination as priests at historic Florida ordination in Sarasota on Feb. 6, 2010

Assembly Participates in Historic Ordination in Sarasota, Florida, Feb. 6, 2010. Bishop Bridget Mary Meehan presides at diaconate ordination of Mary Ellen Sheehan, seated in front, and Judy Lee, seated at podium, Suzanne Thiel right of Meehan

Chapter Four:
The Roman Catholic Women Priests Movement Grows

In 2002, seven women were ordained on the Danube River in Europe. In 2005, nine women were ordained in North America on the St. Lawrence River. In 2006 in Pittsburgh, twelve women were ordained, also on a river. In 2010, there are 80 women in the United States who are ordained or on the path to ordination. Worldwide, there are more than one hundred.

In the Southern region, we have grown from three to fourteen women in two years. This includes two candidates from South America whose identities must be protected. The first three priests in our Region were Eleonora Marinaro, Judith A.B. Lee, and Janice Sevre-Duszynska.

Eleonora Marinaro
In 2007, Dr. Eleonora Marinaro from Port Richey, Florida, who was ordained in the Old Catholic Church, and who had a spiritual counseling practice, was ordained in New York City as a Roman Catholic priest. Eleonora and her husband, David Gabhoury, conduct healing liturgies with communities in Port Richey, Florida. Eleonora is presently also our Region's Program Coordinator, guiding our candidates toward the priesthood with patience, humor, and wisdom. For more information, contact Eleonora/Elly at elly@helpwithdreams.com

Katy Zatsick

Katy Zatsick, who was ordained a Roman Catholic Woman priest on Feb. 6, 2010, is in the process of relocating to Brandon, Florida. After Katy fell and broke her leg in four places, she entered a rehabilitation facility in Brandon and is presently engaged in a ministry of prayerful presence for patients and staff. Her story is in the section about the historic Florida ordinations. Her background information is in the section about the historic Florida ordination. Her contact information is katyrcwp@gmail.com

Deacon

Mary Ellen Sheehan was ordained a Roman Catholic Womandeacon on Feb. 6, 2010. Her background information is in the section about the historic Florida ordinations.

Candidates and Applicants:

Presently, we have three candidates in our region and two catacomb candidates from South America and a number of applicants. We look forward to celebrating many ordinations of qualified women in our Southern Region. For more information, contact Eleonora Marinaro at elly@helpwithdreams.com
or Judy Lee at judyabl@embarqmail.com

Our First Priest in Scotland

On Oct. 24th, 2009, I ordained Morag Liebert a priest in a historic ceremony in the city of Edinburgh, Scotland. Morag has a M.A. in biblical studies and moral philosophy, a post-graduate degree in education, and a B.D. with honors in Divinity. She has been a member of Catholic Women's Ordination for fifteen years. Morag has worked as a volunteer for the past eight years with an organization which helps abused women.. Rev. Frances Forshaw, an Episcopalian priest in the Scottish Episcopal Church, who is part of the clergy team at St. Ninian's Cathedral in Perth, and Rev. Louise Mc Clements, an ordained minister from the local area, participated in the ordination ceremony. Morag presides at liturgies in her home. She is a member of our

Europe-West region. For more information, contact Morag at moragl@connectfree.co.uk

Bishops, according to the original Structures Document ratified in 2007, are ordained to serve the community in pastoral, liturgical, and spiritual roles. A primary function is to ordain qualified candidates in their respective regions. They have no administrative functions and they are not "in charge" of surpervising or "the boss" of anyone. In our non-hierchichal ecclesial system, there is no "head" with authority greater than another; there is a circle in which we all have distinct roles. We work by consensus and by team work. After prayer and discernment by the members of the region, I was elected as their bishop. As Bishop, I am a valued member of the team, no more and no less. Read more about the historic ceremony in chapter 15: A Bishop's Prayer for the Church. My contact information is sofiabmm@aol.com or www.marymotherofjesus.org

Historic Florida Ordinations: 2009-2010

One of the highlights of my first year as Bishop was the historic Florida ordinations. On Dec. 5, 2009, Mary Mother of Jesus community hosted the first ordinations in St. Andrew Church, which was decorated with lush green, red berry wreaths and a lit Christmas tree. It was a beautiful sight to behold. Joining us were members of our sister-church, the Good Shepherd Inclusive Catholic Community in Ft. Myers, with their RCWP pastor, Judy Lee. Dena O'Callaghan and Katy Zatsick, the Ordinands for the Diaconate, were accompanied by their families and friends. Jack Duffy and Michael Rigdon led the community in singing 'Veni Sancte Spiritus' and the Litany of the Saints as the women lay prostrate before the altar in an act of consecration of their ministries to God. I laid hands on both women, followed by the members of the community. After the liturgy, all present gathered for a reception.

Then, on Feb. 6th, 2010, we celebrated the priestly ordinations of Dena and Katy and the diaconate ordination of Mary Ellen Sheehan from Georgia. These women had the educational background and ministerial experience that prepared them for ordination. Dena has a Masters of Divinity degree, and Katy, an M.A. in Pastoral Studies. Dena and her husband, John, a retired Roman Catholic priest, co-pastor a house church in Ocala, Florida. Katy has worked as a hospice chaplain and a pastoral minister and has served the homeless in Lexington, Kentucky. She has recently moved to the Tampa area to be closer to her family and hopes to serve a local community in this area. Mary Ellen Sheehan earned a Masters of Divinity Degree at Notre Dame. She has worked with battered women in shelters in the Atlanta area and is presently an educator.

At the ordination ceremony, Dena shared that she had prepared for this day for a long time. "I was convinced that I was called by God to become a priest. Consequently, I prepared academically, theologically, spiritually, and pastorally. But the obstacles of an exclusively male-dominated hierarchy did not allow me to say 'Yes' to God. A year ago my journey led me to the Roman Catholic Women Priests Movement through Bridget Mary Meehan, bishop. Today, Feb. 6. 2010, after 35 years of waiting, my 'YES' to God will resound for all to hear."

During the moving ceremony, I saw a number of women who had tears streaming down their cheeks. Several said afterwards that they had waited all their lives to witness the ordination of women in the Catholic Church. It was a dream that now had come true.

Bishop Bridget Mary Meehan ordains women as priests at historic ordinations in Sarasota, Fl. on Feb., 6, 2010

power by their presence and support of our ordinations. Pat Ferkenhoff, a member of a local parish in Sarasota, Florida, was quoted in the *Herald Tribune* article as saying: "Well, I'm not going to get my head chopped off or be burned at the stake ("Church Disapproval Doesn't Deter Crowd," *Herald Tribune*, by Anna Scott, Feb.7, 2010).

The Vatican Threaten Catholics With Additional Excommunication

Sarasota, FL, United States (AHN) – "The Vatican has threatened to excommunicate Catholics who support the ordination of the first women priests and deacon in Florida by an excommunicated former nun. Bridget Mary Meehan, one of the bishops of the breakaway Catholic group Roman Catholic Women Priests (RCWP) and who performed the ordination, also received the warning in letters sent by the local diocese in Venice." Read more: http://www.allheadlinenews.com/articles/7017834179#ixzz142fRF Mti

This article stated that Catholics who attended the ordination ceremony at the St. Andrew United Church of Christ in Sarasota will be automatically excommunicated. "They were banned from participating in church sacraments until they are forgiven by a priest."

My Response to Vatican Decree of Excommunication: Disbelief

When I was informed that the Vatican announced on "All Headline News" that Catholics who attended our Florida ordinations were automatically excommunicated, I could not believe it! First: We did not receive a letter from the Vatican or from our local bishop before these ordinations as this news article seems to imply. Second, I am not an ex-nun; I am a Sister for Christian Community, a new form of religious life that is independent of Vatican control and rules and that is dedicated to promoting spiritual unity among all God's people. The prayer of Jesus, "that all may be one," is our motto. Talking about piling on punishments! What was so special about our ordinations in Sarasota that caused the Vatican to react immediately? Yet, this Vatican statement offers immediate forgiveness for Catholics who repent by confessing their sin privately to a priest. So, perhaps, it was like a slap on the wrist, a rather mild punishment! Of course, this is not a problem for women priests and for the people of

God who support us. The Vatican has done their worst by excommunicating us. The oppression of women will not stand because our God is a God of equality. In the end, justice for women in the church and in society will triumph. The Roman Catholic Women Priests Movement is ordaining qualified candidates to serve the people of God because we love our church. As we serve marginalized, alienated, and faithful Catholics who have called us to be their priests in people-empowered, non-hierarchical, inclusive communities, we are following our consciences.

The Catholic Church teaches the primacy of conscience. Bishop Kevin Dowling of Rustenburg, South Africa, in a talk published by the *National Catholic Reporter,* July 25, 2010, quotes Joseph Ratzinger (now Pope Benedict XVI) in his Commentary on the documents of Vatican II, Herder and Herder, 1967:

"Over the pope as expression of the binding claim of ecclesiastical authority, there stands one's own conscience, which must be obeyed before all else, even if necessary against the requirements of ecclesiastical authority." Bishop Dowling states: "we must find an attitude of respect and reverence for difference and diversity as we search for a living unity in the church; that people be allowed, indeed enabled, to find or create the type of community which is expressive of their faith and aspirations concerning their Christian and Catholic lives and engagement in church and world..."

It is ironic and sad to read about the meeting of the Irish bishops with Pope Benedict in February 2010. None of the Irish bishops were fired for the coverup of sexual abuse of youth. Not one bishop in Ireland or elsewhere in the ever broadening global sexual abuse scandal has been excommunicated for their handling of the pedophilia crisis which has destroyed the lives of Catholic children! Yet, the Vatican threatens faithful Catholics who support Roman Catholic Women Priests with excommunication.

The Vatican has a long history of excommunicating, interdicting, and punishing people in one century and canonizing them in another century. Pope Benedict canonized Mother Theodore Guerin, an excommunicated nun in 2005, and canonized Mother Mary MacKillop, another excommunicated nun on October 17, 2010. She was excommunicated as a punishment for exposing a pedophile

Irish priest. Perhaps, Pope Benedict is making excommunication a possible fast track to canonization! Excommunicated Catholics, including Roman Catholic Women Priests, and Clergy sexual abuse survivors and their family members can look to Mother Mary MacKillop as a patron saint, a heavenly friend and companion who walks in solidarity with us in our struggle for justice, reform, and transparency in the contemporary church.

Mary Ward, a foundress of a religious order modeled on the Jesuits, was vilified by church authorities. She was imprisoned at one point and recently has been declared Venerable, a step on the path to sainthood. Of course, we cannot forget St. Joan of Arc, patron of France, who rejected giving assent to church authorities and followed her conscience. She was burned at the stake and later declared a saint! St. Thomas Aquinas, one of the church's greatest theologians, who was censured by the Archbishop of Paris, upheld the primacy of conscience. Thomas rejected Peter Lombard's *Sentences,* a moral theology treatise, which taught that one should not follow one's conscience when it violated church teaching. On the contrary, Aquinas affirmed that "we ought to die excommunicated rather than violate our conscience" (Scriptum super libros Sententiarum, IV,38,2.4 q..a 3; See also IV.27.1.2.q.a.4ad 3; IV.27,3.3. expositio, quoted in Fr. Joe Borg's blog "We ought to died excommunicated rather than violate our conscience").

The Church has also condemned creative visionaries, innovative thinkers, and church reformers such as Galileo, Meister Eckhart, Teresa of Avila, and John Courtney Murray. Today, the Vatican admits its errors and affirms these women and men of intellect, integrity, and courage. One day, the Vatican will affirm women priests as faithful members of the church and even use our inclusive liturgies!

However, at this time, Roman Catholic Women Priests, who confront patriarchy and the abuse of power and sexism in the institutional church, trigger a profound fear in ecclesiastical leaders. This has led to our excommunication and the excommunication of our supporters. But, at the end of the day, I believe that justice, equality, goodness, and truth will prevail. So, Roman Catholic Women Priests and the supporters of our movement, including those brave Catholics who attended the Florida ordinations, are in good company. A holy band of women and men who have gone before us are walking with us nowand supporting us with their prayers as we work creatively and lovingly for a more holy and just church.

In his essay, "Does excommunication do any good?", Rod Modras concludes that excommunication is an embarrassment to most U.S. Catholics and a scandal to non-Catholics. He stated: "I first began thinking about excommunication when friends of mine attended the ordination of two women in the Roman Catholic Women Priests movement in February in Sarasota, Fla. I pointed out to them after the fact that the Florida papers quoted the local bishop as saying that Catholics who participated in the event were excommunicated. The response of my friends, both of whom are weekly communicants, was a dismissive wave of the hand. 'Oh, just like that abortion case in Brazil, where everyone was excommunicated except the rapist'" (*National Catholic Reporter,* July 9, 2010, p.19).

As my brother, Sean, once reminded me, Roman Catholic Women Priests and our supporters should be grateful that we do not live in medieval times because we would be "crispy critters!" However, the church that condemns is also the church that canonizes. Viva Joan of Arc, saint of heretics, St.Theodore Guerin, and St. Mary MacKillop, champions of conscience and models for women and men who are excommunicated like Roman Catholic Women Priests and our supporters. No punishment by church officials will stop the work of the Spirit for a renewed priestly ministry in a community of equals in our time!

Response to Vatican Punishments:
"Latae Sententiae" and "delicta graviora"
When I first heard that Roman Catholic Women Priests had received a "latae" from the Vatican, the first image that crossed my mind was a latte, an expresso with a foamy, milky topping. Let's see- "delicta;" how about something delicious to eat with the "latae"! Obviously, as you guessed by now, I am not a Latin scholar. Neither of these two Latin terms has anything to do with nurturing body or soul!

On May 29, 2008, the Vatican Sacred Congregation for the Doctrine of the Faith issued a decree that the "women priests and the bishops who ordain them would be excommunicated latae

sententiae," which meant automatically. Our movement rejected the penalty of excommunication. "Roman Catholic Women Priests are faithful members of the church who stand in the prophetic tradition of holy disobedience to an unjust law that discriminates against women" (See full response on
http://www.romancatholicwomen priests.org).

Vatican's Declaration Shocks the World

On July 15, 2010, the Vatican declared the ordination of women a grave crime. The ordination of women appeared on the list of the most serious crimes against Roman Catholic canon law, or "delicta graviora" – putting it in the same category as sexual abuse of children by priests - according to Vatican Information Service:
http://visnews-en.blogspot.com/2010/07/publication-of-cdf-norms-on-most.html

These new rules state that the attempted ordination of women is a "grave crime" subject to the same set of procedures and punishments that apply to sexual abuse.

"The rules, which cover the canonical procedures and penalties for the most serious sacramental and moral crimes, were issued as the Vatican confronts one of the worst scandals in recent history: revelations of hundreds of new cases of priests who raped and sodomized children, bishops who covered up for them, and Vatican officials who stood by passively for decades" (Associated Press, Nicole Winfield, "Vatican Revises Its Rules on Clerical Sex Abuse" 07/16/2010:
http://www.gmanews.tv/story/196211/vatican-revises-rules-on-clerical-sex-abuse).

Roman Catholic Women Priests Response to Vatican Declaring Women's Ordination a Crime: Demand Women's Full Equality

"The Roman Catholic Women Priests Movement responded to the Vatican's decree equating women's ordination with pedophilia by priests, by demanding the Vatican affirm women's full equality in the church including priestly ministry.""We demand an end to misogyny in the Catholic Church. We demand that the Vatican adopt reforms to transform church laws and practices to reflect transparency, accountability, justice and equality for all" (See full response on http://www.romancatholicwomen priests.org).

South African Bishop Desmond Tutu, one of the great prophets of justice and equality in our times, preached at the funeral of Steve Biko, a murdered activist from King William's Township on September 25, 1977. He proclaimed to 15,000 mourners and to the world that apartheid was morally bankrupt. "The powers of injustice, of oppression, of exploitation, have done their worst, and they have lost. They have lost because they are immoral and wrong, and our God...is a God of justice and liberation and goodness. Our cause...must triumph because it is moral and just and right." Sixteen years later, institutionalized racism ended in that country (Alex Perry, "The Laughing Bishop," *TIME*, Oct. 11, 2010, p. 42).When the Vatican declared that the ordination of women was a crime against the sacraments and placed it in the same category as pedophilia, also a crime but against morality, the outcry from Catholics and others was immediate. The *Sensus Fidelium*, or, the "Sense of the Faithful," became clear. We reached a tipping point that turned on an outpouring of support for justice for women in the church. The articles below are a small sample of this overflowing tide that is rising from the ocean of God's goodness and dream for women as equals and partners in ushering in the kindom of God in our time. As Bishop Tutu shared, justice always triumphs. So too, justice for women in the Roman Catholic Church will prevail because this cause is God's cause. No matter what the Vatican has done to penalize us, the result has been the growth of our movement, as more support and more women step up to serve in a renewed priestly ministry in inclusive Catholic communities. From this positive view that turns oppression upside down, as God promised through the prophets, we should rejoice and laugh because this reversal is happening to us, too. I sometimes joke: "The Vatican is the gift that keeps on giving."

Worldwide Press Coverage Moves Us On

Here some of the articles that have been pivotal in gaining attention for the growing movement for justice and equality for women in the church.

Since the Vatican declared the attempted ordination of a woman a crime, I was interviewed by *ABC World News, BBC, Irish Times, The*

Nationalist, New York Times, TIME Magazine, The Washington Examiner, and Yoladies.com. My footage of the first ordination of bishops in the United States appeared on *CNN American Morning.* Several radio programs interviewed me in Ireland and the U.S. In addition, other Roman Catholic Women Priests were also interviewed. Here are a few examples of the media coverage:

"Robes for Women"
by Tim Padgett/Ft. Myers, TIME magazine, September 27, 2010
"Like any good priest, Judy Lee knows how to use a Bible story. One of the readings for Roman Catholic Masses on a recent Sunday, from the Book of Wisdom, recounts how the Hebrews defied the pharaoh by worshipping God "in secret." That passage resonates at the house in Fort Myers, Fla., where Lee is conducting Mass for 25 Catholics gathered in front of a coffee-table altar in defiance of the Pope. "Rome says you'll be thrown out of the church for being here," says Lee, "because I'm a woman." "We're the Rosa Parks of the Catholic Church," says Bridget Mary Meehan,...We no longer accept second-class status in our own religion..."
http://www.time.com/time/magazine/article/0,9171,2019635,00.html

"Rise and Revolt: Catholic Women Take on the Vatican,"
YoLadies.com, September 25, 2010 by Kim Milata-Daniels
"Today, there is <u>a growing number of women</u> all over the world who intend to reclaim their once revered place in the church. Since 2002, they have been ordained deacons, priests, and bishops...

"What these women are finding, in their disobedience to unjust laws, is that they are gaining support from Catholics every day. After the Sarasota Diocese warned their members that anyone in attendance of <u>this ordination ceremony</u> would be excommunicated, many showed up stating that they didn't care. It was almost a dare from the backwards, medieval and increasingly irrelevant entity, and one that many were thrilled to take...Jesus was a major rule breaker," Bridget Mary points out to her critics. To those who state that women cannot be leaders because the twelve apostles were all men, she cries foul. It isn't true that there were only twelve apostles - the number was symbolic of the twelve tribes of Israel and nothing more.

http://www.yoladies.com/featured/2010/09/rise-and-revolt---catholic-women-take-on-the-vatican.html

"Credo: Bridget Mary Meehan"
by Leah Fabel, Washington Examiner, September 26, 2010:
Bridget Mary Meehan entered a convent as an 18-year-old woman, inspired by a Roman Catholic faith born during her childhood in the Irish countryside. But as her faith matured, Meehan felt increasingly called to the priesthood, despite church laws forbidding women's ordination Meehan...spoke with *The Washington Examiner* about the beliefs that drive her to disobey the Vatican, even as she holds fast to Catholicism."
http://www.washingtonexaminer.com/local/Bridget-Mary-Meehan-984250-103728309.html#ixzz10bMj7mCD

"Women in Priestly Garb Sounds 'a Great Echo'"
by Elisabetta Povoled, New York Times, September 25, 2010
"Equating ordination of women with a crime like pedophilia drew howls of outrage from many Catholics..."
    "We were excommunicated in 2008, but we rejected it," said Bridget Mary Meehan, a spokeswoman for the Roman Catholic Women Priests organization, who was ordained a priest in 2006 without Vatican consent. "What matters is that we follow our conscience."
http://www.nytimes.com/2010/09/24/world/europe/24milan.html

"Female Bishop Calls for Pope's Resignation"
by Michael Tracey, The Laois Nationalist' Ireland, Aug. 24, 2010
"Meet the first Irish woman bishop since the 5th century, who just happens to be from Laois.... Most Catholics don't know that for 1,200 years, women were deacons, priests and bishops... In the Celtic tradition there was a monastic model of partnership, married and celibate in these double monasteries." In response to Vatican's role in global sexual abuse scandal: "...the Vatican has acted like a crime family...What other church would get away with hiding criminals?"

Read More:

http://www.laois-nationalist.ie/tabId/153/itemId/4221/Female-bishop-calls-for-Popes-resignation.aspx

Catholic Priests Speak Out for Justice for Women in the Church

United States:
"Referring to mentoring the now Rev. Alta Jacko, an esteemed African American elder in the Roman Catholic Church and a lawyer, a parent and a grandparent, Rev. Bossie observed: "I did it because she asked me, because she's very thoughtful," Bossie says. "When someone you like and respect asks you, you try to do it... If God called me, why wouldn't God call a woman?"
http://www.time.com/time/nation/article/0,8599,2021519,00.html
#ixzz10gGwgSpX

Ireland:
"Raising the issues of the need for change in the role of women in the church, the equality of the baptized, and justice for priests falsely accused of abuse, three hundred Irish priests attended the inaugural meeting of the Association of Irish Priests in Portlaoise, County Laois on September 15, 2010. They pledged to campaign for a church which is not governed by a clerical elite but recognised the equality of all members."
http://www.irishtimes.com/newspaper/ireland/2010/0916/12242
78993367.html

Irish Grandmother Calls for Mass Boycott in Ireland:
"An Irish grandmother in her eighties and a mother of a priest, Mrs. Sleeman started a campaign to have parishioners vote with their feet on the matter of women priests.

"It seemed there were organizations and people protesting all over the place, and the idea came to me of a boycott of Mass for one Sunday (September 26th) to draw all these voices together. Let empty pews give the powers-that-be in the church the message that women are no longer happy to be second-class citizens...Why is the church so afraid of women, and especially their ordination? My hope is that empty pews on September 26th will move the hearts and

minds of those in charge, that change will happen, and that the church will emerge invigorated by the equality of all."
http://www.irishtimes.com/newspaper/opinion/2010/0921/1224
279367336.html

Indeed Mrs. Sleeman's day of protest caught on world-wide.

Women Raise Awareness of Church's Unjust Treatment of Women in Rally in USA
"Several hundred Catholics met in Portland, Oregon on Sept. 26, 2010 to pray and to raise awareness of the church's unjust and unequal treatment of women. This event was sponsored by One Spirit-One Call and inspired by Jennifer Sleeman's call for a boycott of Mass on Sep. 26th in Ireland."
http://www.onespiritonecall.org/

Boycott of Mass in Ireland: A Wake-Up Call to Sexism in Church
"Soline Humbert, founder of the organization Brothers and Sisters In Christ, which argues for the ordination of women priests, said ..."She hoped the call to boycott might serve as a wake-up call to encourage people to see the "sexism" in the church, which she said was anathema to the teachings of Christ and the spirit of the Eucharist...We are so used to the sexism in the church we don't see it. We are excluding one section of the community. Sexism is about exclusion. It is not the message of Christ."

Read More:
http://www.irishtimes.com/newspaper/ireland/2010/0927/12242
79760727.html

Bridget Mary Meehan administers the Sacrament of the Anointing of the Sick to her Dad, Jack Meehan at House Church liturgy in Venice, Florida

Chapter Six:
There Have Always Been Women Priests

Roman Catholic Women Priests are reclaiming the ancient heritage of ordained ministry in the Catholic Church. Jesus offered an example of Gospel equality that led to the practice of ordaining women as deacons, priests and bishops in the early church. Jesus treated women and men as equals and partners. Jesus chose the Samaritan woman to announce the good news to her entire village, and the Samaritans accepted Jesus as Messiah because of her testimony.

Mary of Magdala, the first witness to the resurrection, was commissioned by Jesus to be the apostle to the apostles (*John 20:1-18*). In the Gnostic writings, The Gospel of Mary and The Gospel of Philip, Mary of Magdala is portrayed as a threat to Peter because of her authoritative teaching and her close relationship with Christ.

In 1976, the Pontifical Biblical Commission echoed the sentiments of Jesus in concluding there is no biblical reason to prohibit women's ordination. Women and men are created in God's image and both may represent Christ as priests. "In the image of God, God created humankind, male and female God created them" (*Genesis 1:26-27*).

Although the Roman Catholic leadership has been all-male for the past 900 years, Christianity's first millennium saw numerous women serving with distinction as deacons, priests, and bishops. Phoebe, the deacon, was praised by St. Paul for her leadership of the church of Cenchreae (*Romans 16:1-2*). St. Paul identifies Junia as a senior in the faith to himself and labels Junia and her husband, Andronicus, as "outstanding apostles" (*Romans 16:7*). Mary, the mother of John Mark, led a congregation (*Acts 12:12*) and Prisca and Aquila, a married couple, were missionary apostles and coworkers with Paul. Romans uses the word *eklesia* ("church") to describe the group that gathered in their home. "Greet also the church in their house" (*Romans 16:3-5*).

In the Catacomb of St. Priscilla is a fresco dated about 350 A.D. that depicts a woman deacon in the center vested in a dalmatic, her arms raised in the orans position for public worship. On the left side of the scene is a woman being ordained a priest by a bishop seated in a chair. She is vested in an alb, chasuble, and amice, and is holding a gospel scroll. The woman on the right end of this fresco is wearing the same robe as the bishop on the left and is sitting in the same type of chair. She is turned toward the figures in the center and left, watching the woman deacon and priest.

"These attributes," comments Roman Catholic archaeologist and theologian Dorothy Irvin, "indicate that she is thought of as a bishop, while the baby she is holding identifies her as Mary...Women's ordination, however, was based on succession from the apostles, including women such as Mary, the mother of Jesus, Mary from Magdala, Phoebe, Petronella, and others about whose status among the founders of the church there could be no doubt."

Dr. Irvin points to further evidence of women serving as priests: * In the Catacombs of Priscilla, Rome, the fresco "Fractio Panis" shows a group of women "conducting a Eucharistic banquet."

A fourth century floor mosaic covering the tomb of Guilia Runa, located in the cathedral at Annaba acknowledges: "Guilia Runa, woman priest." This cathedral was made famous by St. Augustine of Hippo.

In the catacomb of St. Januarus in Naples, Bitalia, a woman priest is depicted attired in a red chasuble and celebrating the Eucharist. She has two cups on a white cloth in front of her; one is wine and one is water to mix with the wine as is still done today. Above her are two open books with markers, and on each of the four pages the name of an evangelist is written.

Bishop Theodora, mother of Pope Paschal 1, is depicted in a group portrait standing next to St. Praxedis and the Blessed Virgin Mary in a mosaic in a side chapel of the church of St. Praxedis in Rome (*Joan Morris and Ute Eisen*). Theodora, about 820 A.D., and St. Praxedis, who lived seven hundred years earlier, are depicted as standing together, wearing their episcopal crosses. They witness to a conscious connection between women church office holders and Mary, Mother of Jesus.

In their scholarly book, *Ordained Women in Early Church*, Kevin Madigan and Carolyn Osiek conclude that "While the preponderance of evidence for female deacons is in the east, the evidence for women presbyters is greater in the west."

In 494 A.D., Pope Gelasius wrote a letter to the bishops of three regions of southern Italy complaining about the practice of women presiding at the liturgy: "Nevertheless we have heard to our annoyance that divine affairs have come to such a low state that women are encouraged to officiate at the sacred altars, and to take part in all matters imputed to the offices of the male sex, to which they do not belong."

In *Praying with Celtic Holy Women*, I wrote that The Irish <u>Life of Brigit</u> describes the episcopal ordination of St. Brigit of Kildare by Bishop Mel of Ardagh in fifth century Ireland. The evidence in the Celtic Church indicates that women and men were equals in preaching the Gospel, presiding at Mass, and at the other sacraments. Historian Peter Ellis wrote that in the sixth century, three Roman bishops at Tours wrote a letter to two Breton priests, Lovocat and Cathern, expressing their outrage that women were allowed to preside at Eucharist. In mixed-gender monasteries, men and women worked as equals. However, the overall authority within a double monastery often resided with an abbess. St. Brigit selected Conleth to help her administer Kildare, and they governed "their church by a mutual, happy alliance."

The tradition of a Christian seeking a spiritual guide, mentor, or "soul friend" was a prevalent Celtic custom. Women as well as men served as spiritual friends. This custom eventually influenced the entire Church and led to the institutionalizing of private confession. There are stories of spiritual seekers coming to Saint Ita and Saint Samthann to reveal their sins and to receive forgiveness and guidance.

In the tenth century, Bishop Atto of Vercelli wrote that because of the needs of the church, devout women were ordained to lead worship and to preside over the church. Church historian Gary Macy writes, "For over 1200 years the question of the validity of women's ordination remained at least an open question. Some popes, bishops and scholars accepted such ordinations as equal to those of men; others did not."

Thus, we have come full circle. Roman Catholic Women Priests in the 21st century are walking in the footsteps of our sisters in the Gospel and in the early church.

The research of numerous people was compiled for the writing of this chapter.For the serious student of the historical role of women in the Roman Catholic Church, I list the works of some scholars and church historians who have shed much light on the topic.

Brock, Ann Graham, *Mary Magdalene, the First Apostle The Struggle for Authority*, 2003 (quotes Hippolytus (DeCantico 24-26, CSCO 264) pp. 43-49)

Davies, Oliver (ed), *Celtic Spirituality*, New York: Paulist, 1999.

Eisen, Ute, *Women Officeholders in Early Christianity: Epigraphical and Literary Studies*. Collegeville, MN, Liturgical Press, 2000. Transl. From German original.

Ellis, Peter. *Celtic Women*, Grand Rapids, Michigan, Wm. B. Eerdmans Publishing Company, 1996.

Irvin, Dorothy, Roman Catholic theologian and archaeologist; Dorothy is the creator of a series of annual calendars depicting the archaeology of women's traditional ministries in the Church. Contact Dr. Irvin at irvincalendar@hotmail.com

Macy, Gary. *The Hidden History of Women's Ordination*, Oxford, Oxford University Press, 2008.

Macy, Gary. *Theological Studies,* (September. 2000) cited in *Church Watch,* (January-February 2001) p. 3.

Madigan, Kevin and Osiek, Carolyn. *Ordained Women in the Early Church*: A Documentary History, John Hopkins University Press, 2005.

Meehan, Bridget Mary. *Praying with Celtic Holy Women,* Liguori Missouri, Liguori Publications, 2003. (now available on online retailers like amazon.com)*This book was one of five books dropped by Liguori after my ordination in 2006.

Meehan, Bridget Mary. *Praying with Women of the Bible,* Liguori Missouri, Liguori Publications, 1998 (now available on online retailers like amazon.com)*This book was one of five books dropped by Liguori after my ordination in 2006.

Morris, Joan; *The Lady Was A Bishop:* The Hidden History of Women with Clerical Ordination and the Jurisdiction of Bishops; New York: The Macmillan Company; London: Collier-Macmillan Limited, 1973.

Otranto, Giorgi, *Notes on the Female Priesthood in Antiquity,* Section 1.

Raming, Ida; *The Priestly Office of Women:* God's Gift to a Renewed Church, In the series: A History of Women in Ordination, edited by Bernard Cooke and Gary Macy, The Scarecrow Press, Lanham, MD, Toronto, Oxford, 2004.

*I previously published this article, "There have always been Women Priests."

Bridget Mary Meehan presiding at liturgy at Mary Mother of Jesus

Chapter Seven:
The Case for Women Priests: A Brief History and Overview

Recent scholarship affirms that women were ordained in the first thousand years of the church's history. The first half of the church's history provides us with images and accounts of the inclusion of women in Holy Orders that contradict the later prohibition. We are reclaiming this important tradition in order to bring equality and balance, reconciliation, and renewal to the church we love and to all the holy people of God who have been hurt, marginalized, and ostracized in the name of Jesus Christ, who always and everywhere said, as we do, that ALL ARE WELCOME.

"You have given me a reason to return to the church," a woman named Kathy emailed in response to the news that twelve more women would be ordained as Roman Catholic priests in Pittsburgh on July 31, 2006.

This particular reformation began when a bishop of uncommon courage and conscience agreed to ordain seven women priests. The ordination took place June 21, 2002 on the boat, "Passau," floating down the Danube. The Vatican promptly excommunicated the women priests.

Shortly thereafter, a male Roman Catholic bishop, in full apostolic succession, agreed to ordain two of the women priests, Christine Mayr-Lumetzberger and Gisela Forster, as Roman Catholic Bishops. The male bishop granted this ordination in the presence of witnesses, but otherwise in secrecy to avoid reprisal from the Vatican.

In Jan. 2004, Patricia Fresen was ordained by the same male bishop and by Christine Mayr-Lumetzberger and Gisela Forster. The male Roman Catholic bishop told Patricia that day: "We are not doing this for you, but so that justice can be served in our church."

The reason behind wanting to have women ordained as bishops is so that they, in turn, can ordain priests without risk to the many male bishops who, while sympathetic to the cause of women in the clergy, risk excommunication by the Vatican for their participation. Bishop Patricia Fresen explains the rationale for ordination in apostolic succession is that we claim equal rights by using equal rites:

"The main point about our claim to be ordained in apostolic succession is not that we believe that apostolic succession goes back to the apostles, nor that it passes on in some mechanistic way the power to 'confect' the Eucharist and not even that it is the only possible valid form of ordination. The main point from the beginning of RCWP was, in fact, to claim equality for women in the church and to bring about change in the Roman Catholic Church with regard to the ordination of women. This meant, from the beginning, that we needed to be ordained in exactly the same way as men. It is the official church that regards ordination by a bishop in apostolic succession as the only valid form of ordination in the RC church – and therefore there was a need to use the same process if we were to claim equality with male priests and the validity of Orders"(Patricia Fresen, "Response to Rosemary Reuther' Article on Apostolic Succession," published in *National Catholic Reporter*, September 2010).

Six women were ordained as deacons in June 2004 on the ship, "Sissi," on the Danube. More ordinations followed in 2005, with one French woman ordained to the priesthood on a boat on the Saone, near Lyons. On July 25, 2005, nine women were ordained on international waters on the St. Lawrence Seaway. On June 24th, 2006, three women were ordained priests and one woman was ordained a deacon on Lake Constance between Germany, Austria, and Switzerland.

Continuing the line of succession from the apostles, the newly consecrated women bishops ordained Ida Raming. Together, bishops Gisela Forster, Patricia Fresen, and Ida Raming presided over the ordination of the women priests and deacons on the boat in Pittsburgh.

Why all the boats? It just seems fitting. Jesus' first disciples were fishermen. Jesus did some of his best work from the bow of boat, and it was in a boat that he taught his disciples how to weather storms. Water itself is the source and maintainer of life. In 2007 and 2008, other Christian denominations, including one Jewish synagogue, provided hospitality to women priests by opening their sacred spaces for our ordinations and worship. One of the wonderful spiritual blessings that women priests have experienced is the opportunity for dialogue and worship with believers from a variety of religious traditions.

In the organization Roman Catholic Women Priests, we see our ministry specifically designed to reach out to those who, like Kathy, have been alienated, hurt, or rejected by the institutional Catholic Church. There are legions of women who feel like second-class citizens in their own church: divorced and remarried Catholics, gays and lesbians, and all those on the margins of church and society. We minister everywhere we find a need for God's compassion and love. The world is our parish.

As a global congregation, we have come full circle. In the early church, the community gathered in home churches for the celebration of the Eucharist. Romans 16 uses the word *eklesia* ("church") to describe the group that gathered in the home of Prisca and Aquila, a husband-wife ministry team, who were missionary apostles and coworkers with Paul. "Greet Prisca and Aquila who work with me in Christ Jesus, and who risked their necks for my life, to whom not only I give thanks, but also all the churches of the Gentiles. Greet also the church in their house" (*Romans 16:3-5*).

And we're right back there today, and we are part of a growing phenomenon. Many people seek a more individualized, personalized, and caring church community where they can share their faith issues and spiritual journey. According to recent surveys, a major shift is underway in how we worship in Christian denominations. Between six and twelve million Americans worship in house churches where the community shares their faith and prays for each other's concerns. Instead of professionalizing the ministry, the focus is on the gifts of the Spirit in the people of God. All of the baptized are called and receive gifts of the Spirit to build up the Body of Christ. In this context, "pastoring" is a verb, and to pastor one another is to nurture and support the mutual spiritual growth in the context of a faith community. Like Prisca, Lydia, Mary, mother of John Mark, and many other women who led worship in their homes in the early church, women priests often celebrate liturgies in their homes. From 2006-2008, I presided at Eucharist in our mobile home in Florida in the winter. From 2006-2010, I presided at Eucharist in our home in Virginia in the summer. Groups of up to 30 people met in my home to celebrate Mass. In the intimate setting of a living room circle, we shared dialogue homilies, prayed openly for each other's intentions, and extended arms in blessing as we recited the words of consecration together during the Eucharistic Prayer. Here, we experienced the extravagant love of Christ's presence in the sacred meal and in one another. Often, Catholics who experienced the Mass in the warmth of a community found the spiritual home they had been seeking.

Whether ministering in home churches, hospices, college chapels, local street ministries with the poor, or any other place, Roman Catholic Women Priests offer a vision of an inclusive church where *all are welcome* at God's table of plenty at the Banquet of Love. We offer a new model of priestly ministry in which all people and all ministries are equally valued. This is why I don't use a title. We are family. So, when people inquire what they should call me, my response is, "Bridget Mary." I see myself as a sister, a companion on the journey of living fully and loving passionately in the heart of God. As sisters and brothers, partners and equals, a community of believers, we pray, share, worship, and work together for the reign of God's shalom, peace, mercy, compassion, and justice in our world.

It is not enough to ordain women into a patriarchal and hierarchical structure. The clerical structure needs to be changed from a dominator-model with powers reserved only for the clergy into an open, participatory model that honors the gifts of God in the people of God. The present gap between clergy and lay people needs to be eliminated. We need to move from an unaccountable top-down, hierarchy to a people-empowered discipleship of equals. We advocate a community model of ministry based on uniting with the people with whom we serve.

The goal of the Roman Catholic Women Priests community is to bring about the full equality of women in the Roman Catholic

Church. The movement Roman Catholic Women Priests does not perceive itself as a counter-current movement against the Roman Catholic Church. It wants neither a schism nor a break from the Roman Catholic Church but rather wants to work positively within the Church. We invite our Roman Catholic Church leaders to join us in an open, respectful dialogue so that together we may serve the church faithfully and lovingly.

In her address, "Prophetic Obedience: The Experience and Vision of Roman Catholic Women Priests" to the Southeast Pennsylvania Women's Ordination Conference in March, 2005, Bishop Patricia Fresen, D.Th., said: "Now we in the Church are on another 'long walk to freedom,' this time freedom from sexism, from unjust discrimination against women in the church, freedom from oppression by the privileged clerical caste in the church. Once again, we need to stand together in protest, to break the unjust laws because we cannot wait forever, and we need, at least at the beginning, to move into the structures that exist, and change them."

In a church and a world where women are second-class citizens because of their gender, and in a world where women too often suffer from the ravages of violence, war, and poverty, women priests make a positive contribution. Women priests share women's experiences and claim women's power. In my view, it is important to affirm women as free moral agents who make decisions about their bodies and reproductive health in light of primacy of conscience. I believe that our church should be pro-life and pro-woman. All life is precious from womb to grave. The bottom line is to ask ourselves in each situation, in each relationship, what would Jesus do? I believe the answer leads us to loving in the heart of God. Sometimes the path is challenging, but we are never alone. One day, a young woman in the military services who was deeply troubled came to me and told me that she was contemplating an abortion because the doctor said that her baby would be born deformed. She asked what she should do. After listening to her story, I shared my loving support and asked her to consider getting a second opinion, and then making the most loving decisionas she discerned God, who loved her and her unborn baby with infinite tenderness, speaking in the depths of her soul. A year later, she returned with her son, an adorable toddler.

The fact is that women priests are the real deal. We are women from many different backgrounds, interests, cultures, and life experiences. We offer all of this on the altar of our lives as we serve with God's beloved people. I believe that on a deeply spiritual and mystical level, women priests are beginning a healing process in the church of centuries-old deep misogyny in which spiritual power was invested exclusively in men, because they alone could represent Jesus as priests in the Catholic Church. God's loving presence is now embodied in women as images of God, and that is changing everything!

Women priests are reminders that women are equal images of God and that God has a feminine face. This is why I think so many women weep when they attend our liturgies. Some tell us that they have waited all their lives to see a woman preside at Mass and to hear language in our liturgies that is inclusive, rather than exclusive. In most Catholic liturgies, God is referred to with exclusive male imagery, and the use of male pronouns are not only employed for God, but also used to describe human experience. In contrast, here are a few phrases that I sometimes use in liturgies: "We begin our liturgy in the name of God, Source of all being, in the name of Jesus, our brother, in the name of the Spirit, our liberator; let us join hands and hearts as we pray the prayer Jesus taught us: God, our father and mother...."

Roman Catholic Women Priests, in inclusive grassroots communities, are moving the church to honor women's experiences and claim women's power. For some, like the Catholic hierarchy, it is a shakeup and a revolution. Indeed, I believe that we are offering a whole new paradigm that is the work of the Spirit in our time.

Christine Gudorf named the spiritual power at the heart of clericalism when she wrote in 1987, "limitation of sacramental administration to men functions as a claim for men that they- not women- have exclusive power to create and sustain real life, spiritual life through representing Jesus, the source of life. This claim implements a separation between ordinary natural life nurtured by women and spiritual life nurtured by a male elite who serve as symbols for all men" (Christine E. Gudorf, "the Power to Create Sacraments and Men's Need to Brith," *Horizons* 14/2 pp.296-309, quote is from 297).

Sadly, men's claim to the spiritual power to create sacraments is at the heart of misogyny. It is enshrined in the canon law of the church.

In obedience to the Gospel of Jesus, we are disobeying an unjust law that discriminates against women. Canon 1024 states that only a baptized male may receive Holy Orders. This is in contradiction to Canon 849 which states that Baptism is the gateway to the sacraments, which includes Holy Orders. Baptism is the foundation for the validity of Holy Orders, not male gender.

Thus, Canon 1024 denies full membership to women in the church and contradicts Canon 849 which opens all the sacraments to all members of the church. In other words, the sacrament of Baptism makes us equals in Christ. (This argument is presented in the scholarly work of Roman Catholic Woman priest, Raming, Ida; *The Priestly Office of Women: God's Gift to a Renewed Church*, In the series: *A History of Women in Ordination*, edited by Bernard Cooke and Gary Macy, The Scarecrow Press, Lanham, MD, Toronto, Oxford, 2004.)

St. Paul taught, "As many of you as were baptized into Christ have clothed yourselves with Christ. There is no longer Jew or Greek, there no longer servant or free, there is no longer male and female; for all of you are one in Christ Jesus" (*Galatians 3:28*).

For 1200 years, some popes, bishops, and scholars accepted women's ordination as equal to men's. In the 10th century, Bishop Atto of Vercelli wrote about the early church practice of ordaining women to preside over the churches because of the great need. In 1976, The Pontifical Biblical Commission concluded that there is no biblical reason to prohibit women's ordination.

Pope John Paul II contradicted the early tradition of women in priestly ministry when he wrote: "The church has no authority whatsoever to confer priestly ordination on women and...this judgment is to be definitively held by all the Church's faithful."

However, Pope John Paul II did not consult the people of God (including the theologians and the bishops) before issuing this decree.

The church teaches that infallible teaching must reflect the sense of the faithful. Therefore, this teaching is not infallible because it does not reflect the *sensus fidelium*, the faith of the believing community. In fact, according to recent surveys, about 70 percent of Catholics approve of women's ordination, including some of the world's bishops. The church cannot continue to discriminate against women and blame God for it.

People ask, "But what of your vows of obedience?" To a child, obedience is doing what you are told. For an adult, obedience is discerning and following God's direction for our lives. Roman Catholic Women Priests do not take a vow of obedience to a bishop. Our obedience is to the Gospel as we discern together God's guidance for our community.

In our contemporary world, one in three women earn more than their husbands in the U.S. alone; therefore, it is simply mind-boggling that Pope Benedict held up St. Hildegard as a role model because she demonstrated "total obedience to the ecclesiastical authorities."

This is an outragous example of co-opting a courageous reformer who confronted popes and bishops about the corruption of church authorities. Reproving Pope Anastasius IV, St. Hildegard wrote, "Wherefore, O man, you who sit on the papal throne, you despise God when you embrace evil. For in failing to speak out against the evil of those in your company, you are certainly not rejecting evil. Rather you are kissing it. And so the whole world is being led astray through unstable error, simply because people love that which God cast down" (*The Letters of Hildegard of Bingen*, Vol.1 Translated by Joseph L. Baird and Raid K. Ehrman, New York, Oxford Press, 1994). In addition, Hildegard refused to obey the local bishop who ordered that an excommunicated man who was buried in her cemetery be exhumed. As punishment, the bishop placed her monastery under interdict, which meant that the Sisters could not receive sacraments or sing the divine office. Now, does Hildegard sound like a model of submission to ecclesiastical authority, or a role model for courageous reformers in our church to confront church authorities to live Gospel justice and equality?

Lisa Miller concludes that the church has always been threatened by strong women, and in our modern world the hierarchy is still out of touch with reality as women have broken glass ceilings in many professions. Miller states, "…it feels archaic to hold values of submission and obedience above conscience, independence and achievement" (Lisa Miller, Not a Weak Creature", *Newsweek*, Oct 18, 2010, p.21).

When the pope or church authorities re-write the history of courageous women in our church, we must speak up and reclaim our heroines. This is the reason I wrote *Praying with Visionary Women, Praying with Celtic Women, and Praying with Women of the Bible*. On these pages, you will meet soul sisters who loved deeply, who served generously, who faced incredible obstacles, who challenged unjust structures, and who walked in faith and in faithfulness to the Gospel. They inspire us on our way to be imaginative visionaries, creative healers, and courageous prophets. We are walking in sacred footsteps of strong holy women! By reclaiming our ancient spiritual heritage, women priests are shaping a more inclusive, Christ-centered, and Spirit-empowered church of equals in the 21st century.

*The material in this chapter is adapted from an article that I published, "The Case for Women Priests."

Address on Church Reform at Humbert School, Castlebar, County Mayo, Ireland on Aug. 20, 2010:
Jesus' Example of Gospel Equality
In the Gospels, Jesus affirms women's bodies as holy and offers a path to women's equality. According to Jewish cultic law, menstruation was a time of uncleanness. The story of the risk-taking woman with a hemorrhage (recorded in all Synoptic Gospels: Mk 5:25; Lk.8:43-48, Mt.9:20-22) reveals a woman's dignity as a person in the face of religious and social discrimination. She is a model of courage; she is a shaker and a mover who takes decisive action and assumes personal responsibility for her healing. Her journey to wholeness challenges her society's blood taboo. In a world where too many women are still second class citizens (two-thirds of the world's poor are women) and in a church that defends discrimination against half its membership, Jesus confronts the religious-cultic mindsets that stigmatize women because of their femaleness. Jesus calls this gutsy lady who pushed her way through the crowd to touch him, "My Daughter" and tells her that it is <u>her faith</u> that has brought about her healing. In this encounter Jesus not only heals the woman of her pain of rejection, but <u>repudiates the purification rituals of the law-bound religious structures of all time that oppress and discriminate against women</u>. This bold woman's story inspires us

even <u>in seemingly impossible circumstances</u> to seek liberation from second-class status in society and in our church and to claim our empowerment!

As St. Paul reminds us in Galations: 3:28, "in Christ, there is neither male nor female, all are one." Women are equal images of God. Therefore, women are fully capable of representing Christ at the altar. There is no need for a natural resemblance to men, as the Vatican asserts. This is theological nonsense, plain and simple.

Roman Catholic Womnepriests are living Jesus' example of Gospel equality now. When we preside at the altar, we are visible reminders that women are equal images of God and that God has a feminine face.

We are at the forefront of a model of service that offers Catholics a renewed priestly ministry in partnership with the people with whom we serve. The voice of the Catholic people---the sensus fidelium---has spoken. Our communities are growing and, in spite of the threat of excommunication, people flock to our ordinations. The Catholic people have accepted us as their priests, and they continue to support us as we grow from the seven bold women first ordained on the Danube River in 2002 to over 100 now. Ordained women are already ministering in over 23 states across the United States as well as in Canada, Scotland, France, Germany, Austria, and in South America.

Apostolic Succession: Female Priests Ordained Same Way as Men to Claim Equality and Validity of Orders

Roman Catholic Women Priests have broken the Church's Canon Law 1024, an unjust law that discriminates against women. In order to change an unjust law, one must break it as the civil rights and other human rights movements have demonstrated. Despite what some bishops may lead the faithful to believe, our ordinations are valid because we are ordained in the line of apostolic succession within the Roman Catholic Church. Our female priests are ordained in apostolic succession, the same way as men, in order to claim equality and validity of orders. Our first bishops were ordained by a male bishop with apostolic succession. His identity is kept secret to protect him from the wrath of the Vatican!

In some ways, the outrage following the Vatican's announcement listing women's ordination as a serious crime against the sacraments similar to pedophila has been a wake up call for Catholics, especially Catholic women, that the Church is indeed a toxic place for them. From Catholics like Maureen Dowd who writes for the *New York Times* to nuns in India, the outcry has been heard around the world. We have received more requests for inclusive womenpriest led liturgies as well as numerous requests for media interviews.

Global Sex Abuse Crisis Loss of Credibility for Hierarchy Opportunity for Reform and Renewal

Today, Catholics live in a time when the institutional church has lost all credibility because of the cover-up of a global sex abuse scandal, which, like a rapidly spreading cancer, is destroying the moral fiber of our church.

In Ireland, Catholics support the new priests reform movement as an important step forward. Catholics must demand justice for survivors of sexual abuse and justice for women as partners and equals in our church.

The Vatican's new guidelines that extend the statue of limitations for ten years and that streamline cases of sexual abuse in the church court system are mere window-dressing, but do not indicate significant change.

First: All allegations of sexual abuse must be reported to civil authorities whether required by law or not.

Second: The Statue of limitations must be removed. In the U.S., the bishops oppose any extension of these Statues.

Third: The bishops who shuffled predator clergy from parish to parish must be removed and held accountable. When will the Vatican drain the swamp that leads to its own front door?

Our church can no longer appear to be a global crime network! Read the excerpt from Judge Sheila O'Brien's article, "Excommunicate me, please," from the *Chicago Tribune*:

"The Vatican must take full responsibility for the sexual abuse crisis. They should stop blaming the media. According to a recent story, a priest exorcist even claims that the devil is roaming around the Vatican!"

Our institutional church is obviously in free fall. The Vatican has lost all credibility. Abuse of power is at the heart of the global sexual abuse crisis and is also on display in the attempted oppression and suppression of faithful Catholic reform groups, including the U.S.

nuns. These desperate actions by the hierarchy are counterproductive and will ultimately fail.

Catholics: Take Back Church to Reform and Renew it

It is the people of God, including male and female priests and reform-minded bishops, in grassroots communities who must adopt the reforms and "be" the change that we want to see happen in order to revitalize the church as a vibrant, relevant community of believers who live the Gospel in our contemporary world. It is time for Catholics who love our faith to take back our church to reform and renew it!

In conclusion, Roman Catholic Women Priests are faithful members of our church. We are not leaving the Catholic Church; we are leading the church into a new era of equality for women. Like Rosa Parks who refused to sit in the back of the bus, we will not accept second class membership in our church. No Vatican punishment will stop our movement! With the help of God, our heavenly Mother and Father, we will endure and justice will triumph!

The good news is that the birthing process has already begun. Together, we are dreaming a new renewed church into being as we live Gospel equality now, loving in the Heart of God.

Sister Regina Madonna Oliver Presents Bridget Mary for Ordination as a
Priest at Historic U.S. Ordinations on July 31, 2006.

Chapter Eight:
Forever Loved, Forever Loving: The Essence of Theology for Pastoral Care of One Another

In this and the following chapters, we turn to the theology and spirituality based in Jesus' Great Commandment: to love God and to love one another. Loving in the Heart of God is my call to the priesthood.

Our lives are a mystical journey accompanied by the Beloved, who loves us totally and passionately. This is an unearned love, gratuitous, and unconditional—the gracious *gratis* of our Divine Parent, our Forever Friend. In our being and our becoming, God affirms us throughout life. In the book of Genesis, both in the first Creation story (Gen 1:28-31) and in God's covenant with Noah (Gen 8:8-17), God reveals that human beings are the peak of creation; we are called to be the glory of God in the world, but also to be responsible for its well-being.

Indeed, today's thinkers articulate a growing awareness of the interconnectedness of all created things, showing the interdependence of ecology, psychology, theology, and spirituality. Cultural historian Thomas Berry calls this "the New Story." Like all things *new*, however, we find his insights a rediscovery and reiteration of more ancient awareness, as found in the religious sensitivity and response to nature present in Native American and Celtic cultures. For us, Berry is able to coherently illustrate something that is being sensed by the current generation: that the God-given role of human beings is to respect and care for the earth and all her creatures. Whether I savor Berry's insights, or thrill to the earthy music of Celtic pipe, or vibrate to the rhythm of the drumbeat of a rain dance, this awareness arrives at the same point. We know that we are a significant part of a created whole and, therefore, integral to—not separate nor apart from—all that surrounds us, from one another, from those Jesus calls —the least of these⎯—nor are we even separate from the Architect of it all. Whether we use massive telescopes which can scan our galaxy and even detect other galaxies or search the skies with our limited human vision, we are bound to stand in awe in the glow of the brilliant night sky. We can't help but ponder, just as others have done before us, the immensity and complexity of the created universe, and the awesomeness of our charge to be its caretakers. The reality is that God may succeed in luring us to be responsible as the ones to whom Creation is entrusted. Through the awesomeness of nature, God draws us into the Heart of love with varying success. Some will respond sooner to the challenge; some, later. Our response will depend upon the goodwill and affirmative choice to love, which is our freely given answer to God, who says, "Come!" as well as to God who waits for each person to say, "Yes!" While we live out our lives attempting to live *up* to God's invitation, let us not be so scandalized by the failures to love that we see in and around us, nor so immobilized by the accumulated evil that amasses into the grossest of social sin, that we lose sight of the Love of God still beaming out amidst the darkness of human error like a lighthouse beacon. The Spirit of God is inventive to the utmost, and the word that goes out [from God] shall not return to me empty (this is God's promise in Isaiah 55:11 in the NRSV).

It shall accomplish that which I purpose, says God, —and succeed in the thing for which I sent it. Judaism's awareness is that Yahweh *is faithful* and Yahweh will triumph! *Ultimately!* The resurrection message of Jesus is the same: God will triumph! But in both traditions, the *meantime* will have its thorniness. The thorniness of life keeps us ever mindful that, in this interim, until God's purpose is fully achieved, evil abounds because of choices made *to not* love. The choice to not love infects and impinges negatively upon our lives. To be blind to this damaging consequence would be the utmost of naivete. The Judeo-Christian answer to the philosophers' quest to understand the coexistence of *good* and *evil* in the world is *not* to propose, as some philosophies and religions have, a dualism in the Creator *nor* dual Creators. It is, rather, to proclaim with Saint John in his epistle, and with the psalmist, and with the insightful rabbis who first scribed in writing their Judaic understanding of God, this conviction: Yahweh, both transcendent and immanent, is All-Good, and the source only of *good!* Evil, the rabbis suggest in Genesis, cannot be explained as the Babylonians did, as the negative side of fickle and humanesque gods. Genesis suggests that *evil* can only be seen in the failure of human beings to choose to live attuned to the Love that creates them as free agents. Contradicting Babylonian mythology, then, the rabbis of the Old Testament present evil as the result of humankind's fragmented efforts to not be the *created* people of a loving God, but *the creators!* Evil comes when humans try to dominate, control, and abuse, imagining that, in doing so, they are godlike! But the *power* of God is creative, freeing, and wholesome. Saint Paul defines the Love that is in and of God in First Corinthians 13:4–8: "Love is patient; love is kind. Love is not jealous, it does not put on airs, and it is not snobbish; it is never rude or self-seeking; it is not prone to anger, nor does it brood over injuries. Love...rejoices in the truth. There is no limit to love's forbearance, to its trust, its hope, its power to endure. Love never fails."

To be independent of the caring, loving, God, to try to be totally self-contained, self-sufficient, and dominating, is then, ironically, to be totally not Godlike! And so the Genesis writers relate the snowballing effect of evil in the world through story: Cain murders Abel; wars proliferate; human beings mistakenly seek the height of heights in Babel. Finally, in the story of Jesus, the New Testament proclaims that the human venture involves the perfect balance of Providence with human freedom and responsibility.

Although Christian theologians have struggled with the mystery of evil, theologizing can only go so far in explaining what is, in fact, a *mystery!* One has only to look at a crucifix to come face to face with the grotesqueness of evil. One has only to visit Dachau or Auschwitz to be reminded of the almost inconceivable depth of depravity in the souls of human beings. No! One has only to read the morning paper, on most days at least, to encounter the ultimately inexplicable reality of evil in its many manifestations. No mental gymnastics by theologian or philosopher has been able to explain to our total satisfaction the presence of evil in a world fashioned by the All-Good God. But, through and with Jesus, Christianity proclaims that God *is total Goodness and Love.* Jesus proclaims in his very living and dying, the goodness of Abba, and the abomination of evil. Jesus confronts evil; and is victorious over it, because Jesus faces it, absorbs its fury, and *overcomes it* – giving back only *love. God's great "Amen" to Jesus' testimony that God is Love* reaches its climax in the Resurrection event! Jesus makes visible to us in the Risen Christ the Goodness that is Abba, who transforms the worst evil every human person fears – death as extinction – into the graphically depicted promise of a transformed, eternal life. And, God lets us see the *Promise* in the Resurrected Christ! What we can't verbalize, we see with eyes of faith. More than that, we *experience* the Living, Risen Christ as present to us, now--guiding us, safeguarding us, and communicating intimately with us! The Resurrection isn't an event of the past that Christians read about with curiosity; it is a Real Person – a real person whom we *experience* in the depths of our being and in our loving relationships with others.

Ultimately, beyond all this explication of our Judeo-Christian grappling with the mystery of why bad things sometimes (often) happen to good people, we get down to the pastoral nitty-gritty. A particular couple turns to the Presider as they stand beside the casket of their dead two-year-old with the grief-stricken query, "Why did God let this happen?" or, "How can God be a good God, and allow this tremendous loss?" And here we are, back to the inexplicable that can only be accepted by a faith that stubbornly clings to the conviction: Our God is a *good* God. Our God will bring good out of every event, no matter how negative. *And,* our God will overcome!

There *will* be joy in the morning. God *will* turn our sorrow into joy. (But right now, the pastoral heart says to the grieving couple: "In this present moment, I understand that you hurt terribly. I hurt *with* you. I cry with you. God cries *with* you. I don't understand why bad things happen; but I *know* and *believe* that God is Love and God is here, with us, in this sadness, telling us: 'Come; cry on my shoulder.'"

One consolation Christians have is the awareness that, in Jesus' *present moment* on Good Friday, Jesus hurt terribly—but continued to proclaim the Goodness of the God he called by a tender name of love and affection, *Abba*.

Stories of Love and Affirmation

We don't get our answers to the *mystery* of God in our lives as much from the intellectual juggling of scholars as from the stories of courageous people we know and admire and from our own lived story, which contain ever so many such victories. We need only look back with remembering and grateful hearts.

For a moment, let us expand the insights of story into a *lived theology* and move from the level of theologizing into a *spirituality of affirming Goodness*. To take this step, I will share some experiences.

A Tale of Two Aunts

Frances Webster, aunt of my friend Regina Madonna Oliver, was in the habit of talking to herself. Sometimes her mumblings would reach an audible volume, and someone in the family would hear her spit these words out at her image in the mirror, "You are so stupid! Just so stupid!" She would enunciate each syllable with such venom that it made anyone within hearing distance wonder if she really thought that badly of herself. This behavior was of concern to everyone—especially her family—because Fran was an incredibly wonderful human being—one of the most self-sacrificing people we ever knew. The eldest of three orphaned sisters, Fran went to business school at the age of thirteen, had taken a job in West Virginia by the age of fifteen, and began supporting her two younger sisters, Ethel, five years her junior, and Aunt Sleet, five years younger yet. From Sleet's teen years until she died of tuberculosis in her forties, Fran, on a meager salary, took care of her financial needs. Fran also shared her room-and-board accommodations with her sister, Regina's mother, during her high-school years, providing for her with a good secondary education.

Later in life, after Regina's mother's divorce, her entrance into the convent, and her brother's marriage, Fran provided the homestead and refuge for Regina's mom to come back to.

Aunt Fran never married, but she was at the heart of family celebrations, always present with seasonal gifts for her nephew and niece and proud of their every accomplishment. She never had harsh things to say of anyone else—only of herself. But, since the recital of negative self-evaluations was habitual for her, we had to wonder how many times during her ninety-two years she had flung maledictions at herself. What impact would this kind of assault have had on her subconscious? What effect would this negative self-image have on her spiritual life and on her relationship with God? We all found her wonderfully lovable, so why couldn't she understand that God felt that way, too?

Molly McCarthy, my aunt, was an equally incredible human being, but she was amazingly affirmative throughout her life—in all circumstances. She seemed to be serenely positive in her interchanges with others and greatly at peace with her own self-worth. Molly would always say, "That's all right, dear. Things will work out all right!" She thought of everyone, including herself, as God-loved and, therefore, as good!

These two aunts, although of quite different backgrounds, were quite fond of each other and got along famously. Now that they are both with God, we wondered if Aunt Fran has reached the bliss of knowing what Aunt Molly already knew—that God loves her enormously.

The telling of these real-life stories shows that we all sometimes tend to see life, ourselves, and others in ways that Love does not intend. Here is the beauty of the Resurrection message:

God, who is totally positive, affirming Love, can transform even the worst person into a lover. And no Christian has any business wallowing in negatives. After all, our Creator God called *all* of creation "very good."

This chapter will also offer some prayer therapies to cure us of any negative thinking that may have crept into our subconscious, because from there it can surreptitiously poison our outlook on ourselves, deaden our hopes for the future, and stunt our ability to dream noble dreams and aspire to great heights. Like a giant ulcer, negative thinking can spiritually bleed us to death without our even knowing what is wrong. For the many people who say, "I'm depressed," is the real problem their struggle against a lifelong influx of negative self-abuse?

A spiritual director was once overheard saying, "How dare we! How dare we speak badly of one whom God made and called "Good"!" So, I offer some models of affirming prayer, which I believe are attuned to God's original heart-response to the miracle of newly formed creatures. The heart of God formed the word of God about the newborn creation of which each person is the epitome of "Good! Very Good!" Our Nurturing God invites us each day to love in the Heart of God. Here, in the depths of divine love, we discover forgiveness, healing, inner peace, and joy.

Susan's Story

Susan, a vibrant, middle-aged woman, broke into tears as she sat in the counselor's office sharing her story. She blamed herself for the difficulties in her marriage. "I am fat, ugly, and undeserving of love, trapped in a relationship going nowhere," she reflected.

After several sessions of prayer for the healing of her negative self-image, during the final meeting Susan was upbeat, saying, "When I opened myself to God's unconditional love, I was able to appreciate my good qualities for the first time, like my sense of humor. Now I see myself as deserving love and giving love. On my bathroom mirror I put a sign that reads, 'I am a beautiful image of my God.' I begin my day by looking into the mirror and repeating this message. Some mornings I even sing it as I shower. I know I have a long way to go, but I am more hopeful. It feels good to have fun together again."

Like Susan and Fran, many of us have absorbed negative input about ourselves over the entire course of our lives. We may have been asked, "Why are you so stupid?" or, "Why can't you be like your brother or sister?" or, we may have been told, "You'll never amount to anything!"

Such hurtful utterances damage our self-esteem on a level we can't even imagine. We even repeat these things to ourselves as a kind of daily negative litany.

Affirmations From Our Roots

The Story of a Misfit

Joseph Benedict Labre was a social outcast whose life was one of begging and poverty. He was born in France, and, very early on, decided that he had a vocation to become a monk. Notwithstanding his most fervent efforts, however, he was forced to leave the Cistercians, the Carthusians, as well as the Trappists. Despite this lack of acceptance because of what his superiors termed his "eccentricities," Joseph was determined to follow a solitary existence in the service of Christ; he did this by living his life on the road, traveling by little-used routes, sleeping in barns or under hedges, and accepting only what was absolutely necessary for his immediate needs. Dirty and dressed in rags, Joseph made his way to Rome, where his appearance inspired contempt from those who saw him. Here he lived without a permanent home, never knowing where his next meal would come from. Under these circumstances, he was always meek and grateful, taking shelter in various nooks and crannies—even in the ruins of the Colosseum—while spending most of his hours in various churches in front of the Blessed Sacrament. Soon, he took off on other pilgrimages—to Germany, Poland, and Campostella—after which he returned to Rome. There he died, and hardly had he been buried than the street children ran through Rome shouting, "The saint is dead! The saint is dead!"

Despite a life of hardship and disappointment, Benedict came to treat his sufferings with an even-tempered and joyful spirit. Here is a man whose faith in Jesus Christ made him free.

His life was motivated by his internal calling: his vocation to follow a life of prayer and solitude. He survived homelessness, rejection, poverty, hunger, and injustice, showing how even harsh external circumstances cannot compromise a sound sense of self.

The Power of Affirmations

As we tune into Divine Wisdom dwelling in our hearts, we often find thoughts and insights that have the power to heal and transform our lives. Maria, a young, single mother, was worried that bad things would happen to her baby. Then one night after tucking in her infant and kissing him goodnight, she closed her eyes and prayed a blessing over him. As she prayed, she saw an image of the Blessed Mother holding her baby and herself close to her breast. Reflecting on this comforting image, Maria realized that God loved her baby more than she or any human parent could. The image of Mary continues to calm Maria. "No matter how hard it is," she reflects, "I know we are not alone; my child and I are held in God's embrace."

God's message of affirming love can come to us in many forms. Some people might see an image. Others might receive the message when a friend places a hand on our shoulder and reminds us that we are special, saying, "You are intelligent and strong," or, "I thank God for your smile." John, who was recovering from an addiction, once shared what happened when friends in a twelve-step program challenged him to discover God's goodness within: "It changed my life," John said. "I no longer saw myself as a miserable, worthless human being. God's amazing grace helped me find inner treasures that had been truly lost. I felt like a new person. It was like a ton of bricks had fallen from my shoulders, and I knew serenity for the first time in my life."

Another of the ways we can discover God's affirming love is by repeating positive messages that we have heard God speak to us in the depths of our souls. Two inspiring mantras are "God is loving me now" and "God is loving *through* me now." One can repeat them often during the day. These affirmations help us realize that God is closer to us than the next breath, and that we can be divine instruments of love in our encounters with other people.

As we go about our routine activities, such as waiting in line at the store, driving around in the car, or doing household chores, the repetition of one of these affirmations renews our confidence in the divine abundance of God's Spirit that is always with us and in us. We really need this all the time, especially when we are tired, hungry, impatient, and burned out.

Finding Your Own Affirmations

You can discover an affirming mantra of your own. Think for a moment of a name that you would like to call God today, and file it in your memory for a minute.

Think of an affirming statement that feels right for you today. Put the two together. Now you have your mantra for the day. You can use this in the same way that some of us were taught to use aspirations in Catholic school or religious-education class. You simply repeat your mantra over and over whenever you think of it during the day. God is within us. This is basic scriptural theology right from the lips of Christ: "Live on in me, as I do in you" (Jn 15:4). Isn't it amazing that this message comes to us as a surprise?

Another Story

Caring for my frail eighty-six-year-old mother during her final days helped me realize how very fragile life is and how important it is to see every moment as a gift. Dad and I prayed that Mom would experience the intimacy of God's love through our loving attention. Watching her weaken and slip away day by day was painful. Mom prayed her rosary daily, no matter how she felt.

Often I sat nearby, just to be in her presence. When I would look into her eyes, in those final days, she seemed so far away; it was almost as if a veil was slowly rising, and Mom was stepping gently into another world. I think God gave her a sneak preview of the magnificent things to come in the heavenly realm.

Throughout her life, Mom had welcomed God—however, whenever, wherever, and in whomever, God came. She opened her home and her heart to so many who needed love and acceptance and a haven from hurt. In her own sickness, dependence, and old age, she discovered God-was-there-for-her, and continued her lifelong practice of blessing God at every turn.

Now that she has crossed over into the radiance of God's Eternity, she is knowing the fullness of all she believed and clung to. As many people who have stood beside a loved one dying can confirm, God speaks to us through suffering, tears, and losses. I have learned much about love that lasts forever by listening to God speak to me in and through Mother's living and dying.

The loss of my mother reminds me that life is short and that I am getting older, too.

Part of me realizes that I am dealing with the death of my younger self. And, part of me feels grateful to be alive, healthy, and enthusiastic about life. I appreciate the gifts of every passing moment that I took for granted for so long: a golden ray of sunlight gilding the kitchen table where we sit for our morning tea, the perfume of daffodils in our garden filling me with a sense of spring and hope, the sounds of the great melodies and toe-tapping music that Dad plays on saxophone and trumpet each day, the taste of fresh Irish scones baking in the oven—the small, everyday things that I was too busy or distracted to notice before. I make time now to savor the treasures that are right now, right here in front of me. All these little things are gifts from the infinite, loving God, reminding me that I am held in the Heart of Love. And, all the little things in your life that you may have allowed to go unnoticed are gifts from the infinite loving God to *you!*

The Always Affirming God

Open your eyes and look around you. What can you see? Hear? Taste? Touch? Smell? What brings you joy? Comfort? Strength? Peace? No matter what passage or stage of life you are in, God is with you, loving you. Why not saturate yourself with this realization by praying a litany of thanks at the beginning and end of each day, naming all the little things that now have become big things for you because you see them as God's personal gifts?

Nothing can separate you from God's love for you. God loves you more than any person ever could. The story goes that when Teresa of Avila was in prayer, she heard God say, "Teresa, if I had never made the world, I would have made it for you." God is saying the same thing to you:

Mary, Frances, Irene, Lucy, Frank, Joe, Sean, Patrick, Latoya, Marta, _____, "...if I had never made the world, I would make it just for you."

Even if you are feeling down or blue, all you have to do to encounter the Love of your life is open yourself up to God, who, like a mother, reaches out to comfort you. Jesus reminded us of the nurturing tenderness in the heart of our God: "Oh, how often have I yearned to gather you together, like a hen gathering her chicks under her wings..." (Mt 23:37). Have you ever realized that God has been mothering you all your life and continues to do so? You can call on God's mothering nature whenever you need it, just as you called your mother whenever you needed her. Call out, crying your need, and expect a loving response.

God loves you through everyone who loves you. Think of all those people who have touched you lovingly during your life: the doctor who assisted at your birth; the nurse who tucked you into your mother's arms; the daddy who stood by through the whole process and welcomed you with a smile of delight as he tucked your baby fingers into his hands and marveled at the perfection of so small a creature; the mother who suckled you, bathed you, changed your diapers, caressed you; brothers and sisters, so much a part of your growth at every moment; playmates and, later, school friends who shared your childhood secrets; teachers whose infinite patience taught you the rudiments of all you know today; and so on through all those who touched your life any time along the way. Think of all of these, one by one. Now you have a litany of the people who have blessed your life, and you can call on God to bless theirs.

Affirming Others With A Compassion Heart

Listening to God's affirming love challenges us to cradle others and shoulder their burdens with a compassionate heart. Sometimes this is easy to do, but other times not. When we are tired or impatient, we may not have the energy to concentrate on another's needs, but a simple breath prayer such as "The Spirit of God fills me" (as you breathe in), and, "I breathe forth the Spirit of God to touch the life of _____" (as you breathe out) can be a simple but effective way of touching another's life. When we are more collected and at peace ourselves, we can pray for others by allowing divine warmth, kindness, and solace to flow through us to all those crying out to us for love. Sometimes we do this by simply listening to another person and affirming the preciousness of that person's being. Being a loving presence for others will lift their spirits and heal their souls. God's affirming love enables us to be beacons of love for our family, friends, and close associates, but it also reveals that God is calling us to be channels of divine peace, love, and justice in the world at large. Often this can be difficult, for it can mean putting our time, energy, money, reputation, even life on the line to help those in need. It can also mean pitching in to transform structures that discriminate and oppress people. Listening to God's affirming love can wake us up to recognize God's love for everyone, especially the marginalized and dispossessed people in our society. Love can enable us to assist communities or groups, such as the Catholic Worker, Network, and Bread for the World, in their activities for peace and justice. Joining with others to live God's reign in our time, we celebrate our human solidarity, our human worth and wonderfulness, and our value before God.

God wants us to internalize the divine value system, so contradictory to the world's. Our God has deposed the mighty from their thrones and raised the lowly to high places, has filled the hungry with good things and sent the rich away empty (Lk. 1:52–53). God values each one of us immeasurably, no matter how other people may calculate our worth, and wants us to love and cherish even those rejected and despised by society. As Jesus taught us, "The truth is, every time you did this for the least of my sisters or brothers, you did it for me" (Mt 25:40). The

90

bottom line: loving our neighbor *is* loving God. Living in God's affirming love means living a life of love and service. It means doing all we can to bring harmony and peace to the world. Each day, we can bring heaven to earth in all we think, say, and do, and we will be judged, according to Jesus, on how well we sow God's love throughout the world. How can we enlarge the reign of God when our own and others' selfishness too often get in the way of our best intentions? We can love, because God has first loved us. God believes in us and empowers us with a passionate Spirit to do even greater things than we could possibly imagine. We do not have to wait until we are perfect. If we did, we would be waiting until one minute after our eternity begins! We simply need to be open to God's healing action within ourselves and, simultaneously, to follow as the Spirit prompts us to intercede and act on behalf of others. As Jesus assured us: "The truth of the matter is, anyone who has faith in me will do the works I do—and *greater* works besides" (Jn 14:12; emphasis added). This is our scriptural affirmation from the very heart of God. So, when people argue that affirming prayer is a very limited form of prayer because they think, "I have so many things wrong with me that if I went about it this way I might not even make it before my deathbed," we must answer, "Yes—if it all depends on us. But the good news is: it doesn't depend on us! At least not on us alone. It depends on the ever-present God *within* us who is always working in every situation, relationship, and event of our lives. Prayer is answeredin ways that surpass our greatest expectations! In God's affirming love, *all things are possible!* All we have to do is open our hearts to our affirming God."

*This Chapter is adapted from *Affirmations from the Heart of God* by Bridget Mary Meehan and Regina Madonna Oliver, originally published in 1998. It is available from online retailers.

Chapter Nine:
Experience Deep Love For God and For Others in the Heart of Love

L iving Christ's call to love God and one another is not easy. Once, in a shared homily a woman said, "I am struck with your message of God's unconditional and deep love for us and for all of creation. I have never known love like that from other people, but I love my children that way and I hope they love me back."

We continue to explore our relationships in the Heart of Love as the essence of Gospel living.

On September 25, 1996, my parents celebrated their golden wedding anniversary. Our family and friends gathered around the table, praised God for Mom and Dad's fifty years, celebrated a liturgy and renewal of marriage vows, and shared a delicious outdoor picnic. Then we sang and danced late into the evening to Irish songs and tunes from the forties. But, the most wonderful memory for me was watching Dad and Mom sitting close together, holding hands and smiling at each other with a warmth of love that lit up the evening sky. In the midst of this party, everyone's eyes were drawn upward to the pinnacle of our roof as granddaughter Katie pointed with a breathless, "Oh, look!" to two doves nestling together. We could feel God's presence embracing us all.

When we encounter the depths of love, we enter the presence of God. One of the most beautiful gifts of life is to experience this kind of spiritual presence. As we love another, we discover the beauty of God's love within us, joining our hearts in a spiritual communion. In our relationships, we learn to listen to one another and share our ideas, feelings, and dreams. We learn to experience the world through another human being's perspective. The experience of intimacy with another energizes and strengthens us to meet life's greatest challenges.

Holocaust survivor and author Victor Frankl credits his survival to the spiritual presence he maintained with his wife during his imprisonment. This relationshipsustained him throughout the darkest days of his life. Frankl recalls, "...as my friend and I stumbled on for miles, slipping on icy spots, supporting each other time and time again, dragging one another up and onward, nothing was said but we both knew: Each of us was thinking of his wife. Occasionally I looked at the sky, where the stars were fading and the pink light of the morning was beginning to spread behind a dark bank of clouds. But my mind clung to my wife's image imagining it with an uncanny acuteness. I heard her answering me, as with her smile and frank and encouraging look. Real or not, her look was then more luminous than the sun which was beginning to rise" (*Man's Search for Meaning*).

One way to experience this spirit-to-spirit connection with others is by initiating a prayerful dialogue with them. We can do this with people who are present and wish to participate in this encounter. For example, couples who have made marriage encounters deepen their relationship by writing love letters to each other on a regular basis. I'll never forget the marriage encounter weekend that my co-worker and friend, Regina, and I made at the urging of a priest-chaplain to enhance our ministry as counselors and planners of marriage-preparation and enrichment programs. We strengthened our friendship that weekend through our sharing. I was touched by the strong and honest feelings the team members expressed about their successes and failures to love as married couples. However, I was deeply moved by the open communication that occurred. It was apparent that some painful issues emerged as couples shared their feelings about their relationships, acting as living sacraments‖ to each other: healing, nurturing, challenging, and loving. The marriage encounter motto is "Love is a decision"; this means that every day, married couples have an opportunity to be lovers in every aspect of their lives, from the time they get up in the morning to the time they retire at night.

Married love reflects the passionate, boundless love in the heart of God inviting human beings everywhere into caring relationships with others. God is love, and God embraces us through other people. In other words, each of us needs other people in our lives, and all of us are created for human community in one form or another. Couples are visible reminders that God's love is tangible, intimate, warm, and tender. All we have to do is reach out in love to others to discover our profound communion with our fellow human beings.

We can also bond with people we love who are unable to talk with us because of separation or various obstacles or blockages. For instance, suppose your relationship with your parents or siblings is still influencing you in a negative way. Maybe you cannot deal with the situation in real life; neither you nor they are capable of discussing the issues at hand because of old emotional wounds that prevent any progress. In the prayer of spiritual presence, however, you can open yourself to them, move beyond present obstacles, and experience healing. The love you experience from this powerful dialogue may indeed lead to the beginning of some brand-new relationships in your life.

Another way you can experience the spiritual presence of another does not involve words but consists of simply focusing on the other with attentive love. As you gently gaze at the other, you can become united with the other person in a deep spiritual union. Words are not needed. By doing this, you can experience a profound spiritual presence capable of transforming your life.

When my mother, Bridie, was eighty-five, she was hospitalized for more than two months with heart and kidney failure as well as serious respiratory problems and life-threatening infections. As I sat by her bedside, holding her hand each day, I felt closer to her than I had in my whole life. It was as if her spirit was dwelling within the depths of my soul. On this level, I realized that nothing, not even death, could separate me from Mom. This enabled me to let go and place Mom in God's eternal embrace, where we are closer than we could have ever imagined or dreamed.

For fifteen years, I worked in pastoral ministry in a small parish on a military post. Part of my job was to develop a pre-marriage program. In this process, I met several times with young engaged couples. I remember one young couple who became teary-eyed as they told me that they were facing a long separation because of military duty. They shared with me their survival plan to make it through this challenging time. They would each wear a locket with a picture inside close to their hearts to remind them that they held each other close, no matter where they were.

One young mother once told me that her favorite time of day was in the evenings when she would rock her toddler to sleep. She shared, "as I hold my beloved child close and sing a lullaby to her, I experience the power of Love that is always within us, surrounding us and filling us with peace."

Several years ago, George and Josephine, a delightful elderly couple, were part of my local small faith community. In spite of serious medical problems, George and Josephine brought a cheerful spirit to our Friday morning gatherings. "Where two or three are gathered in my name, I am there in their midst," Jesus tells us (Matthew 18:20 *Inclusive New Testament*). And so, this little community discovered that one of the best ways to be with the God, who will never abandon us, is to share with one another in the midst of troubles.

One day, Josephine had a stroke. For months, George spent almost every waking moment at her side, helping her in any way he could. After several more months in a rehabilitation center, Josephine came home. George was ecstatic. Now they were together again at home where they belonged. Not long after this, George's cancer worsened. Now it was Josephine who remained by George's side, comforting and strengthening him. Every time I visited them, they shared that the only thing that mattered now was being together, offering their suffering to God, and trusting in God's gracious will. A few months later, George died, and within a year, Josephine passed away. Like a diamond that sparkles more brightly with age, wear, and tender loving care, Josephine and George's love will never die. It is inspiring to me how courageous people like George and Josephine let go in the face of serious physical illness and, in their surrender, find peace in their journey to eternity's shore.

When I did a cable TV production on *The Healing Power of Prayer*, I interviewed George, a physicist who worked in the area of artificial intelligence. George told his story about being in remission from cancer for fourteen years. His cancer had just returned. During the taping, he shared with us how he dialogued with God about his disease. He didn't know why this was happening to him, but he was radiant with joy because in this journey he had encountered so much love in the midst of his illness. George told us that he experienced a vivid sense of God's presence surrounding him. It was like he had one foot in this world and one foot in heaven. He felt like a little excited child who had peeked in the candy store window and couldn't wait to get inside. His smile was contagious, and none of us will ever forget his last words to us: "All of life is gift, oh so many gifts!"

We are precious treasures created in the divine image who long for deep communion with our God. From the moment of our conception, God loves each one intimately, boundlessly, totally, passionately, as if he or she were the only person in the world. In fact, as God revealed to Teresa of Avila, "If I had never made the world, I would make it just for you!"

Like swimming in the shimmering glow of moonlight, we can encounter divine grace lighting our path everywhere. This mystery of divine love surrounds us always. Our whole life is a wonderful journey into the amazing depths of an infinite love that will go on forever. Imagine! Every day God says, "I love you!" All we have to do is open up our spiritual awareness, and we will hear this spoken in many natural ways. Like a fond mother, God is constantly saying, "My dear, dear child, I love you!"

Within this aura of love union, we experience our communion with God and with everyone else. There are no clear boundaries. We can always pray. This is contemplative prayer: being present to the ever-presence of God and to every other person because all beings are enfolded into this energizing force. Contemplative prayer grounds our being in Love and enables us to see the face of God everywhere, even in pain and suffering. We become aware, as George did, that everything is gift.

I have developed a prayerful approach to experience deep love with God and with others.

Prayer Exercises

Opening to Love

Go to a quiet place and relax your body. Begin with your head, face, and neck…release any tension in these areas…relax your shoulders, chest, arms, and hands…release any tension in your back, stomach, hips, legs, and feet. Be aware of your breathing. Inhale and exhale slowly for several minutes. One way to do this is to count to four as you inhale, hold your breath for the count of four, and count to four as you exhale.

Open yourself to the depths of God's love. Allow this boundless love to permeate your entire being. Simply be in the presence of Love…no words are necessary….

Listen to God call you by name and tell you how much you are loved. Be still for a while and immerse yourself in the Divine Presence.

Be aware of any feelings, thoughts, sensations, and images that emerge as you reflect on God's love for you. Share these in a prayer dialogue with God.

Be aware of anyone in your life with whom you want to experience spiritual communion. Share your feelings about this person with God.

Imagine God holding this person close to the Divine Heart.

Imagine God holding both of you in the Divine Embrace.

If you want, enter into a conversation with this person (these people). Be attentive to any feelings, thoughts, sensations, and images that emerge as you reflect on your relationship with her or him (them). Be aware of anything God wants to do to lead you to deeper intimacy. If you wish, record any insights from this encounter in your journal.

Encounter with a Friend or Family Member (Living or Deceased)

Choose someone with whom you are close and want to share deep love. Invite him or her to join you in this experience.

If you are present in the same place, lovingly look at your friend. If the person is not present, form a picture of her or him in your imagination.

Become aware of your spiritual connection with that person.

Share your feelings of gratitude and love for all this person means to you in a prayerful conversation with that person and/or with God.

Encounter with a Challenging Relationship
Choose someone you find difficult to love.

If the person is present, lovingly look at her or him. If the person is not present, form a picture of her or him in your imagination.

Begin a prayerful conversation with that person and/or with God. Share your feelings and thoughts with this person as openly and honestly as possible.

Spend some time, if appropriate, giving and receiving forgiveness.

Become aware of your spiritual bond with this person.

Open yourself to God's healing love in this relationship.

Encounter with a Loved One Who Has Died
Choose a member of your family, a friend, or another significant person who has died and for whom you still grieve.

Form a picture of your loved one in your imagination.

Begin a prayerful conversation with that person. Do not be afraid of expressing feelings of grief, anger, or loss with this person.

Forgive this person for leaving you.

Spend whatever time you need in giving and receiving forgiveness in this relationship.

Surrender this person into God's loving embrace.

Become aware of sharing a deep spiritual communion with the person.

Allow God's love to fill any emptiness or loneliness you still experience.

Encounter with a Special Mentor, Teacher, or Leader
Choose a person who has inspired you, encouraged you, affirmed your gifts, and consoled you in your weakness.

If the person is present, lovingly look at her or him. If the person is not present, form a picture of her or him in your imagination.

Become aware of your spiritual oneness with that person.

Begin a prayerful conversation.

Share your feelings of gratitude with that person for all she or he did to encourage, help, or challenge you.

Now share with this person ways in which you are growing more like her or him in your relationship with others.

Encounters with Jesus, Mary the Mother of Jesus, or a Favorite Mystic or Saint

Whenever we pray to Jesus or with Mary or the mystics or saints, we believe that they are spiritually present to us and are willing to intercede or share their love, joy, hope, faith, passion, strength, and courage with us.

Imagine Jesus, Mary, and/or your favorite mystic or saint with you.

Become aware of your spiritual relationship with them. Become conscious that Jesus, Mary, or your favorite mystic or saint has been ministering to you, loving you, protecting you, and helping you.

Begin a prayerful conversation.

Share your hopes, dreams, anxieties, joys, and failures with them.

Listen to their response to you. Be aware of any images, words, feelings, or insights that describe your experience.

Imagine yourself living in the fullness of God's love with all of humanity and the entire cosmos in their presence.

If a word or phrase comes to mind, you may wish to repeat it as a mantra or prayer phrase.

As you do so, imagine yourself living as a person of passion and justice like Jesus, Mary, or your favorite mystic or saint, in your relationships with others.

*This chapter is adapted from *Praying with a Passionate Heart* by Bridget Mary Meehan and Regina Madonna Oliver, originally published in 1999, pp.1-12, and is available from online retailers.

Chapter Ten:
Live Joyfully and Peacefully Each Day

As young children, my niece, Katie, and nephew, Danny, taught me wonderful ways to live peacefully and joyfully in the present moment. Through their eyes, I caught awe-filled glimpses into the preciousness of life.

Being with these delightful children made me evermore conscious that God is in love with us and probably smiles a lot at our human antics—maybe even bursts out now and again in uproarious laughter.

I remember one sleepover at our house when Katie assigned the roles in our "pretend family": "I'm the mommy, and I'm having twins. Grandpa, you be the daddy; Danny, you are the dog; and Aunt Mary, you're my mommy." She then proceeded to put two small dolls under her shirt and asked, "Who's going to drive me to the hospital?" Of course, I volunteered. Moments later, Katie "gave birth" to babies, Bridget and Patrick. It was amazing to watch her in action. First, shed "give birth" by popping each one out from under her shirt, then she'd cuddle her babies, nurse them, and put them to bed. As she did this, she was totally absorbed in loving her children. As this game progressed, most of the dolls and bears around the house became Katie's "daughters" and "sons."On this particular evening, I think she had about a dozen children! You should have seen the room—we had babies everywhere. Meanwhile, Danny boy crawled around the floor, barking his little heart out.

He took great pride in protecting his sister's babies from monsters. No wonder we did not get to bed until nearly midnight!

If we live like Katie and Danny did as young children—peacefully and joyfully in the present moment—we will encounter the face of God everywhere around us. We will recognize that God comes to us, not only in the happy times—in the new mother cuddling her babies, in the child riding her bike by herself for the first time—but also in the real struggles—in the cancer patient dealing with surgery and chemotherapy, in the unemployed neighbor who loses financial security, in a friend who wrestles with depression, in a teen's rebellion, in a parent's illness.

God is forever loving us and cries within us when we encounter enormous pain and suffering. Corrie ten Boom, a Nazi concentration camp survivor, reminds us that "there is no pit so deep that God's love is not deeper still." This means that no matter what trouble or suffering visits us, God is present, loving us fully in the experience of our deepest pain and losses. At times like these, the soul expands, and the spirit becomes strong. At times like these, we can experience deep peace.

After reading *Angela's Ashes* by Frank McCourt, my father, Jack, observed that this story brought back many memories of the poverty his family endured in the thirties in Ireland. "Yet," he smiled, "I know the human spirit can make it through anything—if love is present. My parents did the best they could. But I was determined that my children would have a better life, and this has given me peace and happiness."

"It has taken me so many years to be at peace in my own skin," Joan, a woman I counseled, told me. Suffering from depression, Joan saw herself as disorganized and sloppy—a failure in everything she tried. Then one day she tried a healing-prayer exercise in which she dialogued with her undesirable parts. In her imagination, Joan sat in front of the fireplace in her living room and invited the Holy One to be with her and her undesirable parts. To her surprise, she saw God embrace her and hold her weaknesses close to the Divine Heart.

"I felt wrapped in a blanket, and warmth spread all over my body," Joan shared, "I've never felt more loved in my life, and for the first time I experienced true inner peace and contentment." The next time I saw Joan, several months had passed. I almost didn't recognize her. She had gone back to school and was embarking on a new career. She had a beautiful new dress and hairstyle. But her smile said it all—here is a radiant, confident, happy woman who knows she is beautiful. Laughter heals the heart. If we can laugh—a real belly laugh—it means we don't take ourselves or our world too seriously. We know thatno matter how silly or ridiculous things are,all shall be well. Laughter reminds us that God loves us more than we can dream and cares for us always. We are never alone.

When our house was next door to a school which has now been torn down and replaced by "McMansions," one of the high points of my day during the warm weather was to sit on our backyard swing with a cup of tea and listen to the children playing and laughing. Once in a while, when a ball came flying over into our yard, I gave myself permission to join in their fun by tossing the ball as high as I could back into the schoolyard.

I used to enjoy babysitting Katie and Danny, my niece and nephew when they were young children. I smile whenever I remember some of these great times. On one school night, my sister-in-law, Nancy, gave me instructions to put the children to bed so that they would be asleep by 9 p.m. My brother simply smiled that knowing, brotherly smile—the one that says, "now it's your turn, Sis."

I did come prepared. I had a plan; I would read them a story, say prayers, and tuck the little darlings into bed at their regular bedtimes. However, when I shared my plan with the children, Katie pleaded, "Just one little game before we go to bed. Please, Aunt Mary, then we'll go to sleep real quick!" And so began a game called "Duck, Duck, Goose, Katie-style." This consisted of a high-speed chase across their bed. Guess who was the goose most of the time? There I was chasing two children, up one side of the bed and down the other, then around the bedroom for several minutes until I collapsed on the floor. If anyone could have observed us, they would have had a hard time figuring out who was having the most fun. I must confess, it felt great to be silly and enjoy the exhilaration of childhood. And I am in good company, since Jesus delighted in being with the children, and reproved his disciples for trying to keep them away from him. "Let the children alone—let them come to me," he chided. "The kingdom of heaven belongs to such as these" (Matthew 19:14 *Inclusive New Testament*).

For several years before she died, my mother, Bridie, was in and out of hospitals with life-threatening ailments.. Several times, the doctors had given up on her. Some days it was a struggle for her to eat, drink, take the amount of medicine prescribed, and do the therapy necessary to keep her mobile. Dad devised a way to get her to exercise. He would play their favorite Irish music and dance with her. She smiled, looking into Dad's eyes, and then slowly moved her feet a little to his rhythmic sway. This was amazing to us because, before this, Mom never liked to dance. But, she did love to be held by her dear Jack. Was God preparing Mom and all of us for the cosmic dance we will be doing with God, the angels and saints, our relatives, and all creation throughout eternity?

It is at moments like these that perhaps we can hear the divine love song that our hearts have always known and tap to the heavenly rhythm that our feet can't forget. When we experience God's peace and joy in our lives, we often expand our images of God. This means that we not only know God's love in a new way, but we feel God's immeasurable tenderness in our hearts. We enter into an intimate relationship with Divine Love. This happened in my spiritual journey. As a young child, I saw God as a watchful judge who focused on my failures. I tried to please the God I loved by living up to the rules—the commandments and laws of the Church. As a teen, I encountered God as Lover. At this time, I focused on developing a close relationship with my Intimate Friend. In recent years, I have discovered God as Mother and as Holy Wisdom. Now, I am exploring the feminine face of God and delighting in the healing and transforming presence of the Divine Feminine in my life. This is leading me to a deeper relationship with a loving God. I now feel more awe, more mystery, more intimacy, more peace, and morejoy than I have ever experienced before in my holy encounters.

Living joyfully and peacefully is not always easy. I remember the panic I felt thirty years ago when the doctor told me that I had a growth on my vocal cords. The doctor recommended a month of voice rest. After the shock wore off, I struggled with my anxieties and wrestled with God. How would things turn out? Would I need surgery? Was this cancer? Would I need to give up my teaching career? I bargained with God and argued with God until I was weary of asking, "Why me? Why now?" In the process, I realized that there were no answers to my questions, but that God was with me, loving me into greater wholeness each day. As time passed by, I began what I call a "soaking prayer." Each day, I would sit on the patio and imagine God's healing love flowing through my entire being. I imagined Jesus embracing me and healing not only my vocal cords, but my fears of cancer and death. At the end of the month, not only had my vocal cords healed, but I had found a new sense of peace and trust that no matter what happened in my life, nothing would separate me from God's love.

No matter what challenges we face, we can find peace and joy everywhere and in every circumstance. The Bible reminds us hundreds of times *not to be afraid!* Yet, how often do we find ourselves worrying about something? I, for one, am a worry expert. I have wasted lots of time being anxious about circumstances beyond my control. Sometimes I'll let go of the situation and give it to God; then, ten minutes later, I'll start fretting about the same thing again. It's at times like these that I imagine God is chuckling at me as I go back and forth with my worry. It will probably take me a lifetime to really get it! But I keep trying. It really is quite simple. All we have to do is open ourselves to receive the gift Jesus wants to give us in every situation in our lives: "Peace, I leave with you, my peace I give to you. I do not give to you as the world gives. Do not let your hearts be troubled, and do not let them be afraid" (John 14:27 *Inclusive* New Testament).

Living joyfully and peacefully involves us in a caring community. Sharing with friends, with family, and with small faith communities provides us with a variety of ways to encourage, support, and love one another. A friend of mine, Maria, who was recently diagnosed with cancer, shared, "I could feel the support in the air before I went for surgery; it was tangible." Thomas Merton, a Cistercian monk and contemporary prophet, believed that spirituality is about being in communion with all creation. Merton used the image of the cosmic dance to describe a consciousness of God's presence in all aspects of life: "When we are alone on a starlit night, when by chance we see the migrating birds in autumn descending on a grove of junipers to rest and eat; when we see children in a moment when they are really children, when we know love in our own hearts...all these provide a glimpse of the cosmic dance."

Saint Paul found the key to happiness is being "...rooted and grounded in love...able to grasp fully the breadth, length, height and depth of Christ's love and, with all God's holy ones, experience this love that surpasses all understanding..." (Ephesians 3:17–19 *Inclusive New Testament*). Teresa of Avila prayed, "O Love that loves me more than I can love myself or understand." We, like Paul and Teresa, can celebrate the infinite, boundless love of God for us and live each day joyfully and peacefully in the Divine Embrace.

Prayer Experiences to Live Joyfully and Peacefully

There are various things each person can do to live more joyfully and peacefully.

• Be aware of the face of God in people you meet when you wait in line. Look around you and *see* the face of God in everyone. Pray for the needs of each person. Bless each person in your heart, and offer thanks for their presence in our world. Ask God to give them their hearts' delights.

• Compose a litany of intercession for those in need of peace, joy, and abundance in their lives. As you read the newspaper or watch the news, pray for the healing of violence, oppression, discrimination, and poverty.

• Volunteer to help those in need. For example, donate your time to at a local shelter, a soup kitchen, a children's program, or a senior citizen group. In a prayer journal, reflect upon your experiences. Ask yourself, how did you encounter God's presence in the people you served? What is God saying to you through these encounters?

• Play with children and experience the exuberance of the child within you as you do so. Or, choose your favorite fun activity and just enjoy it. As you do so, be aware that God is playing with you.

• Go to a funny movie or read a funny book and laugh uproariously. Let the laughter set your spirit free. Let it relax, free, and heal you. Reflect on God as a "Merry God," and a "Joyful God" who is with you in happy and fun times.

• Enjoy a meal, a conversation, or an intimate moment with a loved one. Offer thanks to God and share with this person (or these people) the things you are truly grateful for in your relationship(s).

• Repeat a form of the Jesus Prayer when you are performing ordinary tasks such as showering, working, eating, exercising, or trying to sleep: "Jesus Christ, Child of God, have mercy on me, a sinner"; or, "Jesus, mercy"; or, simply "Jesus" or "mercy." You can synchronize the Jesus Prayer with your breathing in and breathing out; that is, breathe in: "Jesus"; breathe out: "mercy." Repeat the Jesus Prayer for people facing trouble or crisis.

• Recite the rosary, using all your senses to take in the sights, sounds, tastes, and smells of the world around you. One example: as you walk, pray the rosary for the marvels of creation that you see, touch, taste, hear, smell, and so forth.

• Imagine yourself playing with God. Delight fully in the experience; Sing, dance, laugh, and rejoice in God's presence.

• Begin by spending a few minutes breathing deeply. Let go of all distractions and fears; if thoughts or feelings come, simply ignore them and let them float away as a twig floats down a quiet stream on a spring day.Just relax and let yourself enjoy God's love surrounding you; be still and at peace.

Scripture Prayer Encounter

"Thus will you afterward find rest in her, and she will become your joy" SIRACH 6:29 (New American Bible).

In the Hebrew, Greek, and Latin languages, wisdom is of feminine grammatical gender. Wisdom is the feminine aspect of the one God and is personified as a woman in Scripture. Biblical scholars suggest we use the word *Sophia*, a transliteration of the Greek word for 'wisdom', to connote a person and not an abstract mental concept.

Playful Prayer Encounter

Sophia's presence is holy ground. Wherever we are is holy ground. Reflect upon places where you recognize the presence of the feminine face of God.

How can recognizing Sophia's presence bring joy and peace in your life? in our world? How can a sense of intimacy with the Divine Feminine help us become more whole?

Recall a time when you felt dynamic, creative, and full of confidence. What were you doing? Why was the experience so creative for you?

Take several deep breaths. Imagine that with each breath, you begin to release any tension you feel...as you relax more deeply, your mind can become quiet and still. Invite your body to let go completely. Take time to be present to your surroundings...be aware of what your senses experience.

When you feel ready, go to a place where you can enjoy life...take some time to have fun. What are you doing? How are you feeling? Who is with you? Where are you?

Be in awe of yourself...see yourself as a miracle...a reflection of Sophia's loving presence in the world....

Imagine yourself living the life you want to live as a caring, compassionate, vibrant person....Believe that nothing is impossible for you with Sophia's help.

Repeat one of the following prayer phrases, or mantras, to help you focus on Sophia's empowering presence in your life: "Sophia is my joy," "Sophia is my peace," or "Sophia is my delight." You may make up your own.

Be aware of the ordinary events, the daily miracles of your life, such as a warm shower, hot coffee, smiles, friendly greetings from family members or coworkers. Reflect on how these and many other little wonders‖ are holy ground for you….

Light a candle each day in a special place to remind yourself of the hope, peace, and joy that is all around you. Let the light from the candle help you to live the joy of Sophia more fully in the holy ground‖ of life.

A Soaking Prayer in Jesus' Love

"Who will separate us from the love of Christ? Will [trouble], or distress, or persecution, or [hunger], or nakedness, or [danger], or [violence]? For I am convinced that neither death nor angels…nor things present, nor things to come… nor anything else in all creation, will be able to separate us from the love of God in Christ Jesus…."ROMANS 8:35, 38, 39 (New Revised Standard Version Bible).

Before beginning, take a few moments to get comfortable and relaxed. Sit upright in a comfortable chair, feet flat on the floor. Or, lie on a rug or mat. Focus your attention on your breathing for a few minutes….Take a few deep, slow, abdominal breaths…inhale…exhale…inhale…exhale….

Now, close your eyes…relax your body gently by imagining a beautiful golden light starting at the top of your head and moving slowly down your neck, spine, arms, legs, and feet. Experience the warmth from this light filling your body with a feeling of well-being and vitality….

In your imagination, you see a stranger coming toward you….at first, you do not recognize this person…but now you know it is Jesus…he hugs you and holds you closeand sits beside you, holding your hand…Jesus invites you to share your feelings, thoughts, concerns, worries, troubles, or joys with him….Take as much time as you need….

Jesus has already experienced what you are going through and is with you now, loving you with compassion and strength. Experience the affection of Jesus for you. Soak in the healing, transforming love of Jesus for you. Let yourself be loved by Jesus.

Jesus gives you a special gift; share this gift with all those you meet….

You are one with Jesus. You are one with all people and all creation...become love to all those you meet, especially those who are suffering or in crisis...become like Jesus, a radiant reflection of joy and peace....

Go in peace and be joyous, aware that nothing can separate you from the love of Jesus....

*This chapter is adapted from *Praying With a Passionate Heart* by Bridget Mary Meehan and Regina Madonna Oliver, 1999. pp. 13-25. It is available from Online Retailers.

Chapter Eleven:
Share Your Feelings With God

D uring a time of crisis in my life, my spiritual director offered me some wise advice: "Don't be afraid to tell God how angry you feel." God can handle all of your feelings, no matter how negative you may think they are. This began a slow but liberating journey for me. Anger has been a painful emotion for me to acknowledge. However, in recent years, I have learned to share my anger more openly about situations in which I felt I was treated unfairly by others. As I have done so, I have experienced a new sense of closeness with God and a better understanding of myself and other people. When I'm angry, sometimes I'll spend my prayer time complaining to God until I get it all out. At other times, I'll run with my anger. When I express my anger in these ways, I experience God's presence within helping me deal with the situation in a positive, life-giving manner. God is like an understanding friend who reminds me, "I love you as you are, no matter how angry or frustrated you feel. Trust me enough to share your outrage with me."

It is true; God accepts us the way we truly are. There is no need to pretend that we are in control, or that life is fair, or that we have it all together. Our capacity to express our emotions honestly with God deepens our capacity for a passionate relationship with the Holy One. We can reveal to God a less than perfect face—the one with the blemishes and wrinkles that we sometimes cover up in order to hide from others. As we share all of ourselves with God—including our feelings—we will realize that God accepts us as we are and loves us more than we have ever imagined.

Twelve years ago, a friend of mine had a heart attack. She told me later that when she awoke in the intensive care unit of the hospital, the first things she saw were tubes and wires attached all over her body. She felt pain in her chest and started to complain to God: "How could you let this happen to me? I thought you loved me and promised to take care of me. I don't want to die. Please, help me now!" After a while, she drifted into a dreamlike state in which she thought she had died. In this place, she felt completely safe and peaceful. She recalls, "When I awoke, I knew God was very close to me and had answered my prayer. I was no longer afraid to die."

Suffering and human misery are present everywhere we turn. Eighty percent of the world's population lives on 20 percent of its resources. Hunger, poverty, homelessness, and violence are a daily reality for many in the human family. In the United States in 2010, the top 1% of the wealthy controls eighty percent of the nation's wealth. We have consumed more of the earth's resources than most people would consume in several lifetimes. I don't know about you, but I feel guilty. My prayerful struggles with my own guilt have led me to meet with people who feel the same way. We support one another in our efforts to simplify our lives, pray for transformation of unjust structures, and take small, concrete steps to work for change in society. We do simple things like cook meals for shelters, help with hotlines, tutor children, visit the elderly, donate clothes and furniture to the needy in our neighborhoods, and lobby for a more just and inclusive society. It may not seem like a lot, but together we believe we can make a difference. There are no answers to some of life's most painful questions: *Why does a child die? Why do planes crash? Why does a young man in the prime of life get a malignant tumor? Why did the Holocaust and ethnic cleansing in Bosnia destroy millions of lives? Why do thousands die in wars and terrorist attacks throughout the world? Why do bad things happen to good people?*

When we experience loss and suffering, when we have no answers to human pain, sometimes all we can do is come to the cross and weep in the darkness, knowing we are not alone; God weeps with us.

One of the most tender experiences I ever heard about took place at a healing service. The team moved from person to person, laying hands on each one's head, asking what healing the person needed. When the team came to Elaine, she asked for healing of her guilt over a sexual sin that had happened many years ago during her adolescence. Later, Elaine shared her experience: "I closed my eyes and prayed with the team. The image of myself as a young girl after my first sexual encounter came to me. I was lying on my bed. Then I saw Jesus come through my bedroom door. He sat on my bed and looked into my eyes and gently caressed my face. I poured out my guilt and shame until I felt I had gotten it all out of me. He didn't say anything, but I never felt so much love and forgiveness in my life. A tremendous burden was lifted from my shoulders. I feel like a new person now."

One time I was sitting at my computer, focused on completing a chapter in a new manuscript. I heard Katie and Danny running down the steps, giggling and yelling, "Aunt Mary, play with us!" So I stopped. I looked at them. I got up and turned on the music. The three of us did a fast jitterbug around the basement, grabbing dolls, bears, and chairs as extra partners. We were spinning, jumping, and laughing. When the music ended, I was gasping for breath but feeling great. Just then, their daddy arrived to pick them up. They gave me a quick hug and raced up the steps. I went back to my work. Suddenly, it hit me: this is what life in the Spirit is all about—dancing our love with gusto. God invites each of us to participate in the dance of life, where we share our joys and sorrows with one another. Sometimes, when we can let go of our agendas, schedules and work, grace embraces us and swings us around in a moment that leaves us breathless and awe-filled!

When I first met Steve, he was devastated after a bitter divorce from his wife, Monica. According to the custody settlement, he now could see his kids only once a month. In a letter he wrote, "When we were together, our home was filled with fighting, arguments, and turmoil. But I miss my children so much. Most days I feel so sad that I don't even want to get up. Work is my only distraction. I feel so lonely. Even God feels far away from me." In my return letter, I invited him to read the passages in Scripture in which Jesus faced loneliness. Several months went by and I heard from Steve again. He wrote, "The more time I spent sharing my pain with Jesus, the less time I felt sorry for myself. I am now able to look back and stop the blame game. I have been able to forgive Monica and myself. Now I really appreciate every minute I have with my children so much more."

At one point, I made a transition that has changed my life. I wasn't sure where the Spirit was leading, but I had an inkling that my future would involve a new spiritual adventure. At that time I asked God excitedly, "Can I spend the rest of my life savoring your passionate love and sharing it more fully with people everywhere?" I recorded my thoughts and feelings in a prayer journal. This helped me reflect on the Spirit speaking within my heart. Here, I discovered the strength, wisdom, and vitality I needed to pursue this new direction that suddenly unfolded in my life.

Fifteen years ago, my friend Rea suggested, "Bridget, why don't you start a spiritual TV talk show. You could call it *Godtalk*. At first, I thought this would be impossible. I felt like I was stepping off a cliff with no help in sight. But a voice within assured me, Don't be afraid to jump; I'll catch you." So I took the plunge and landed in the arms of Love. I felt as if God had been talking to me through Rea. Doors began to open. I made a phone call to our local cable station and learned that the first step was to take the required classes. Since I was someone who could not even program a VCR/DVD, this was quite a challenge.

Then a group of wonderful volunteers whom I had never met before came into my life to help with the program. Two of these young men, Jay and John, had previous television experience. So, I became a producer/host ready to roll with a series of five programs on *The Healing Power of Prayer*, featuring interviews and prayer experiences on healing mind, body, and spirit, and a new series on courageous women in the Bible and Christian tradition. *Godtalk* was officially launched.

In the story of the two disciples' encounter with the Risen Christ on the road to Emmaus, They said to one another, "Weren't our hearts burning inside us as he talked to us on the road and explained the scriptures to us"‖ (Luke 24:32 *New Revised Standard Version Bible*)? The disciples' souls were stirred in the presence of Everlasting Love accompanying them on their journey. It took them a while, but they finally realized what had happened. God was with them in their sorrow, but they didn't recognize the Stranger walking beside them.

These disciples were slow on the pickup, just like we sometimes are. We don't always understand the events of our lives. We may be frightened or upset. We may be excited or happy. Cant you just see God smiling and laughing when we finally recognize the Stranger who comes to us in a number of disguises on our earthly pilgrimage? Then, our hearts will burn within us, too.

We can express our positive feelings of well-being, happiness, and joy as well as loneliness, sadness, and disappointment in our prayer. In the Bible, we read about Miriam leading the Hebrew women in the dance of liberation in the Exodus story. Dancing for joy is a great way of celebrating life's large and small victories: "Then the prophet Miriam...took a tambourine in her hand, and all the women went out after her with tambourines and with dancing. And Miriam sang to them, 'Sing to God, for the Holy One has triumphed gloriously, horse and rider God has thrown into the sea'" (Exodus 15:20–21 *New Revised Standard Version Bible*). The Book of Psalms (all from the *New Revised Standard Version Bible*) is filled with prayers expressing every emotion under the sun. For example, Psalm 13 expresses the prayer of one in sorrow: "How long shall I harbor sorrow in my soul, grief in my heart day after day" (2)? Psalm 4 expresses joyful trust in God: —You put gladness into my heart, more than when grain and wine abound. As soon as I lie down, I fall peacefully asleep for you alone....bring security to my dwelling‖ (7–8). Psalm 17 voices anger at injustice and asks for deliverance from persecution: "Hear a just cause, O God....hide me in the shadow of your wings from the wicked who despoil me....rise up, O God, confront them, overthrow them" (1, 8–9, 13)! Like the psalmist, we can compose our own passionate prayers, expressing our innermost feelings and desires to God.

The mystics and saints through the ages likewise prayed from their hearts, sharing their deepest emotions with God and with all creation. Francis of Assisi expressed his love for creation in joyful canticles to the earth's creatures, praising God for Brother Sun and Sister Moon. Brigit of Kildare was known for her happy spirit. In this grace she welcomed everyone to her table: "I should like a table of the choicest food for the family of heaven. Let the ale be made from the fruits of faith and the food be forgiving love. I should welcome the poor to my feast, for they are God's children. I should welcome the sick to my feast for they are God's joy. Let the poor sit with Jesus at the highest place, and the sick dance with the angels."

Catherine of Siena, Doctor of the Church, wrote with gratitude about the gift of her close friendship with Raymond of Capua. In a letter to Raymond she says that the foundation of love of neighbor is the love of God, and that love begets a faith that bonds us with another just as she and Raymond are bonded.

Like holy women and men through the ages, we can open ourselves up and share our deepest feelings with God and with others. To sum up, we may want to keep in mind the following:

• First, God loves you and all of your feelings. No feeling is unacceptable to God. Feelings are neither right nor wrong. They are morally neutral. God is big enough to handle all our feelings, even the negative ones like hate, anger, fear, envy, or guilt.

• Second, it is important to share our feelings with God as openly and honestly as we can. God, like our best friend, is a good listener and accepts us and our feelings as they are. Sometimes we may want to use our bodies and minds to express our feelings to God—like jumping for joy, or screaming out loud as we punch our anger out on a pillow. We can also talk out our anxieties by writing a worry list.

• Third, God will heal and transform the hurting areas in our lives if we simply ask and are open to being healed. God will exult over us as we express our joys, our happiness, and our contentment in prayers of praise and thanksgiving.

• Fourth, sometimes we may need to seek professional help to handle deeply painful emotions. This can go hand in hand with the divine therapy that God does in healing the hurting places inside us.

• Fifth, celebrate — *really* celebrate — the love and happiness you experience on earth with all God's creatures. All your feelings are holy ground. Emotions, both negative and positive, can be powerful steppingstones leading you into the heart of God.

Prayer Ways to Share Your Feelings with God

A Guided Prayer Experience for Healing Shame
Use soft instrumental music in the background, and read or tape the prayer suggestions before you begin.

Breathe deeply for several minutes....

As you inhale, be aware of God's love embracing your entire being....

As you exhale, let go of all stress or tension....

Close your eyes and slowly and quietly repeat one of the following words or phrases for several minutes: God, Liberator, Healer, Shaddai, Faithful One, Spirit of Peace, Helper, Comforter.

Remember a time in your life when you experienced shame or guilt. As you recall the situation, be conscious of how you felt...what you did...share your feelings openly and honestly with God....

God is the same yesterday, today, and forever. God can free you now from the guilt of the past and heal you completely now. Invite God to forgive and free you from your guilt and shame....

Imagine God embracing you and healing you...see yourself being filled with warmth and peace...observe God giving you the love and strength you need to become whole — fully alive and in love with God and others....Become a new creation....

Listen to God speak in the depths of your heart...let those words be emblazoned in your soul to remind you of God's tender mercies in your life....

Share your feelings, thoughts, and insights about this experience with God....

In your imagination, do whatever feels comfortable to celebrate God's healing love that you have experienced....

Whenever you feel ready, come back to the room, a lot lighter than before you began this prayer.

A Psalm of Joy

Pray this psalm or compose your own psalm expressing your joy to God:

Great is your compassion, O nurturing God.
You fill us with good things like hot rolls and
coffee each day.
You kiss away the wounds of our hearts.
In our tears and fears we experience
your tender love.

Response: Sing to God for joy.

Wondrous are your marvelous deeds in our lives.
You hold us close to you in tribulation and trial.
You free us from oppression
that we may walk always in the light
of your freedom.

Response: Sing to God for joy.

Tender is your touch and warm is your smile.
You draw us with your transforming grace.
You connect us with one another that we may praise you forever
as one people united in love and committed to service.

Response: Sing to God for joy.

Glorious and gracious is your presence in our world.

You help us care for Earth's creatures,
the fruit of your womb.
You fill us with your wisdom and strength
that we may rejoice with all creation forever
in your presence.

Response: Sing to God for joy.

Praying Your Feelings through Art
Paint, draw, sketch, or use clay to express your feelings.

Look at your drawing, painting, or sketch; spend several minutes breathing in and out your feelings. One way of doing this is the following:

With each breath, take in your feelings....

Breathe in your joy, peace, freedom, anxiety, fear, hate....

As you do so, give your feelings as they are to God....

Praying Your Feelings through Scripture
"My compassion grows warm and tender" HOSEA 11:8 (New Revised Standard Version Bible).

"Peace I leave with you, my peace I give to you. I do not give to you as the world gives. Do not let your hearts be troubled and do not let them be afraid" JOHN 14:27 (New Revised Standard Version Bible).

The symbols, stories, and images of the Bible give us many possibilities for sharing our feelings with God.

Recall that God wants you to experience boundless love, joy, and peace in the Divine Heart. God loves you infinitely, passionately, and totally. Each of us is held close to all those we love in the Divine Heart. Indeed, all the human family is profoundly united in love in God's heart. This wondrous mystery can fill us with awe, wonder, and love. We have nothing to fear.

Quiet yourself. Relax. Breathe in deeply the boundless love of God for you...breathe out deeply God's love for all people and for all creation...breathe in Divine Peace...let go of anxiety and fear...read the Scriptures...listen as God reveals the desires of the Divine Heart for you and for every creature....

Share the desires and feelings of your heart with God....

Compose a litany of thanksgiving or a spontaneous prayer expressing your feelings of gratitude for the gift of God's love and peace in your life. Or offer the following prayer:

"Divine Lover, I rejoice in your passionate love present in me and all around me—everywhere—and in everyone. Hold me close forever to your heart. Here I will discover deep joy and true serenity. Amen."

Pray for all people throughout the world who are in turmoil. As each group comes to mind, imagine them in a large, cosmic heart surrounded by love and peace...see them being transformed by God's love. Now imagine all people and all creation living together in peace, justice, and harmony...what kind of world would this be? Decide on something you can do to make the world a more peaceful place. Perhaps you can begin by performing an act of kindness for a person or creature near you now.

*This chapter is adapted from *Praying With a Passionate Heart* by Bridget Mary Meehan and Regina Madonna Oliver, 1999. Pp.27-39. It is available from Online Retailers.

Chapter Twelve:
Wounded Healers: Celebrating Spiritual Empowerment

To heal we allow ourselves to be healed by Love.

It was one of those beautiful days. The sun was shining brightly. The clouds looked like fluffy white pillows resting on the soft blue bed of the sky. The breeze was warm and gentle. I was opening the window and enjoying the view when the phone rang. It was my friend Sarah on the other end of the line. She told me about a recent family gathering at which her sisters and brothers had spent hours arguing over silly little things that had happened years ago. "By the time it was over," Sarah complained, "I was so annoyed that I just wanted to get out of there. You'd think we'd get along a lot better now that we are adults."

It is not unusual to feel irritated with members of our family or friends or co-workers.

Sometimes it helps to remind ourselves that there are no perfect families.

All of us are wounded and on a journey to wholeness. Yet, love is inside us and all around us, and we can choose to be instruments of peace. When we live in God's love, we have unlimited potential to forgive, heal, encourage, and love others.

When we are held prisoner by anger, resentment, or blaming others, we can't see the forest for the trees. Everything revolves around *our* needs, hurts, and pain. The prayer attributed to the thirteenth-century mystic Saint Francis of Assisi suggests an attitude shift that can set us free: "God, make me an instrument of your peace. Where there is hatred, let me sow love; where there is injury, pardon; where there is sadness, joy." In other words, if we want joy, peace, and happiness, we need to live compassionately.

We cannot change others any more than they can change us. All we can do is love others where they are and support their growth. As Sarah attempted to work on her own spiritual development, she realized that she was becoming a new person. "When I discovered what a struggle it was to change myself, I became more understanding toward my family. I realized that a lot of things that bothered me about them—anger, greed, jealousy—were in me."

This process of unleashing our potential involves a new way of thinking and a deeper way of loving. Young couples think that they have experienced the fullness of love on their wedding day and honeymoon, while in reality they have just planted the seeds that, if carefully tended, will blossom into a magnificent love in the years ahead. Becoming the beloved of another is a lifetime commitment. As we juggle the responsibilities of families and jobs, pursue careers, and nurture relationships, we can become more patient and gentle with ourselves and those around us. After all, we are all works in progress who are becoming the beloved of others.

Like Mary, the Mother of Jesus, and the disciples of Jesus who received the fullness of the Spirit on Pentecost, we too can proclaim the fiery sparks of passionate gospel living every day. When we open ourselves to the Holy Spirit's presence in our lives, miracles can happen. Pentecost is a reality that we can experience every day. The promise of Jesus is the source of our spiritual empowerment: "You will receive power when the Holy Spirit has come upon you, and you will be my witnesses...to the ends of the Earth" (Acts 1:8 *Inclusive New Testament*).

One eve of Pentecost several years ago, my friend Regina and I were traveling on the Southeast Freeway in Washington, D.C., when we heard a loud thud and our car came to a sudden stop. While traffic was speeding by us, we could see a police cruiser pull up right behind us. The officer approached us and asked us what was the matter. "Our wheel fell off," Regina replied. The officer shook his head in disbelief that we had not had a serious accident. Another car stopped behind the cruiser, and a man walked up to us and handed us our tire, which he had chased down the freeway. After thanking both men for helping us, Regina and I praised God for protecting us. The officer smiled and said: "This is amazing grace at work for sure." Then he called ahead for a tow truck and stopped traffic on the busy thruway so that our car could be turned around and towed away. We have told this story to many people over the years. We believe that God's saving power is always with us. We especially need it when we get in a car!

We have often joked about our poor sense of direction—which means that on most trips we get lost at least once. Traveling together, we are a dynamic duo, open to adventure. Our infamous detours remind us that we are not alone. God is very close to us, whether we are on the right or wrong road. Through our meanderings, we have learned to enjoy the present moment of travel as a time of divine encounter. Just as life sometimes takes us in directions that we did not anticipate, we can be at peace if we realize it is all part of God's plan. Regina and I have discovered that when we let go and let God lead us, even our wrong turns become occasions of blessings that can energize us. It causes us to spend more time together, seeking and searching for the right road, and as we do this, God often speaks to us through each other's ideas and insights. Sometimes we dream new dreams and share new visions for religious life or for women's ministry in the Church.

Alice's story reminds me that God uses others to ignite the fire of hope in our hearts. One day, Alice, a woman from our prayer community, confided that her husband had criticized her and contradicted her opinions for years. She made excuses for his behavior: "He only hit me once. It was my fault. I didn't listen to him. I was too preoccupied with the children." After months of therapy, Alice realized that her lack of self-love was a problem. What changed her life was when she realized that she was worthy of love: "I asked God to help me see my potential. Some members of my support group told me that they saw me as intelligent, caring, and a good listener." Their message motivated Alice to go back to school and eventually to become a counselor. Now she leads women's empowerment seminars and works in the area of career transitions and life changes. Hundreds of people have been inspired by Alice's story, and their lives have been enriched by her programs.

Women in our society need to affirm their self-worth and celebrate their empowerment. The media consistently devalues women by sending negative messages about women's bodies and sexuality. When everything we see and hear tells us that women need to look or dress a certain way to attract men, or have certain makeup or clothes to be beautiful, we are being sold a bill of goods that leads to emptiness. Women come in all shapes and sizes. God accepts us as we are and calls us beloved. We need to discover our true identity in the depths of our souls. We are beautiful and gifted because we are created in the image of God. The words of Hildegard of Bingen, the medieval mystic, reflect our nobility and brilliance: "In this circle of earthly existence, you shine with radiant light so finely it surpasses understanding. God hugs you. You are encircled by the arms of the Mystery of God."

Each of us can be messengers of the in-breaking of God's reign. We can discover ways to unleash the Spirit of God's love right where we are. Sometimes it involves visiting a friend who has lost a loved one, or cooking a meal for a sick neighbor, or fixing a leaky faucet for an elderly parent, or smiling at the next person we meet. Sometimes it involves taking risks, such as sharing your vulnerability with others. For me, it has meant sharing my soul journey through books. Ten years ago, if anyone had told me I would have published eighteen books by now, I would have laughed in disbelief and said, "That's impossible!"

Yet, as I opened myself to the Holy Spirit's guidance, it became clear that God was calling me to share with people I'd probably never meet this side of heaven my personal relationship with the loving God who is transforming my life. We can celebrate our spiritual empowerment by being radiant reflections of God to our sisters and brothers in the world. Like Jesus, each of us has been chosen: "The Spirit of God is upon me because the Most High has anointed me to bring good news to those who are poor. God has sent me to proclaim liberty to those held captive and recovery of sight to those who are blind, and release to those in prison—to proclaim the year of Our God's favor" (Luke 4:18–19 *Inclusive New Testament*). By our baptisms, we have been empowered by the Spirit for ministry to others. Jesus reminds us that there is no love for God without love for neighbor. "This is my commandment, love one another as I have loved you" (John 15:12 *Inclusive New Testament*).

We are meant to experience intimacy with God and spiritual empowerment through human relationships. The more we love one another, the more we are energized to love God. Other people are meant to be icons of God's presence, shining brightly like warm sunshine in our lives. Like a flower that blossoms when watered by the spring rain, so our deepest selves grow when someone loves us. Warm human love helps us experience what God's intimate love feels like. If I had never known human tenderness, how could I appreciate God's infinite love?

Yet, human love has its limitations. I can never completely know or be known by another person. Each of us is a mystery—even to ourselves. Only God can love us perfectly. Only God can make up for the love that we needed in our relationships but did not receive. Only God can liberate us from the walls that separate us from others; only God can heal the hurts that fester in the depths of our souls. God's love alone can free, heal, and empower us to love with the freedom of the children of God. Saint Augustine had it right when he recognized the hole in the human heart that could only be filled by the Holy One. It is true indeed, as he said, that our hearts are restless until they rest in God. It is here that we can find our lasting home. God alone can fill the thirsts of the human heart for peace, love, and fulfillment. Jesus invites us to come and drink from the Fountain of Life: "Any who are thirsty, let them come to me and drink! Those who believe in me, as the Scripture says, 'From their innermost being will flow rivers of living water'" (John 7:37–38 *Inclusive New Testament*). What more could we ask for?

This chapter provides three approaches to celebrate your spiritual empowerment. The first one consists of utilizing your intuitive processes to help you tune in to your higher purpose and discover your creative power. In this model, you will create prayers that reflect the Spirit speaking in the depths of your being. The second approach leads you in a contemplative experience of yourself as a new creation. The third approach provides a psalm to celebrate God's Spirit in your life. Prayer approaches like those can help you to celebrate your spiritual empowerment. Each one invites you to open a window through which you can glimpse grace everywhere, every day of your life.

Prayer Experience to Celebrate Spiritual Empowerment

Choose an area in your life in which you desire to lift your spirit higher. Where are you being challenged? Where do you want to take risks? Listen to your inner wisdom and find your creative spirit.

Imagine yourself living as if you have exceeded your expectations....

Discover Your Creative Power

Write a prayer stating your desire to discover your creative power, your inner source of vitality, passion, energy, and life. Some of the ones I use are: "I rise with Beauty, radiant with love"; "I can do all things in God who strengthens me"∥; "Desire of my Soul, empower me"; "Wisdom of God, guide me to challenge injustice."

Repeat your prayer often. This repetition deepens the thought patterns and releases behaviors that raise your awareness of the Spirit speaking in the depths of your being.

When I repeat the words, "I rise with Beauty, radiant with Love," for example, before I begin a speech to a large audience or in front of the television cameras, I become centered, calm, and confident, and I experience God's love energizing me.

Record any thoughts, feelings, insights, images, and intuitions that flow from this prayer experience in painting, poetry, song, dance, clay, or any favorite artistic expression. One time, I turned on praise music and painted the bright colors and feelings of joy and exuberance as I reflected on my creative power. Another time, I danced with my creative spirit. As I swirled and swayed to the music, I experienced the Holy Spirit releasing my inhibitions and leaping within me. Later, as I reflected on this dance, I knew the Spirit was freeing me to connect more with God's Divine Energy within me and around me in the beautiful earth.

Share your creative power with family, friends, neighbors, and even strangers. I often "try on" my new spiritual insights with people who are close to me before I present them to a larger audience at retreats and conferences around the world. This helps me to receive feedback and affirmation. I have discovered that sometimes, those closest to us are wise guides in assisting us in the process of spiritually discerning the new gifts the Spirit brings into our lives. All we have to be is open to the voice of God speaking in those around us.

Experience Yourself As a New Creation

Lie or sit down comfortably, close your eyes, and breathe deeply. Breathe in and out slowly and deeply from the abdomen. As you breathe in and out, be aware of your body. Begin at the top of your head...your face...ears...nose...eyes...mouth...chin....

Move downward, focusing on each body part to the very soles of your feet....Inhale deep breaths and send oxygen to every cell in your body....As you exhale, imagine blowing out any stress, tightness, or pain you find in your body....

As you breathe in and out, imagine the Spirit filling you with love, peace, kindness, self control, gentleness, wisdom, generosity, or whatever your heart desires....

Be aware of any areas in which you need to experience forgiveness, healing, freedom, love....

Invite the Spirit to speak to your heart....Is God calling you to be a new creation, to do great things?...to witness the gospel in a powerful way?...to let go of old resentments and hostilities?...to become the beloved of others?...to live the life of the Spirit in its fullness?...to take some risks for the gospel? Imagine yourself doing great things for God....

Picture yourself loving passionately, acting justly, walking humbly with your God....

Open yourself to the infinite, tender love of God for you....Listen to God praise you for your gifts....

Listen as God calls you by name and expresses gratitude for your gifts (—*your name*, I bless you for reflecting my kindness in your smile...my generosity in your service to the elderly/young/homeless....)

Look into a mirror—either a real or imaginary one—and see yourself as God's beloved, truly possessing everything you need to be peaceful and happy....

As you open yourself to this experience, be aware of any insights, images, feelings, or thoughts that emerge....

Give thanks that you are the handiwork of God... your body is God's special dwelling place...your mind and spirit reflect the thoughts, feelings, and insights of God's Spirit...write a poem, psalm, or prayer of thanksgiving....

Take all the time you need to move your awareness back to the place where you are...when you are ready, open your eyes, stretch your body gently, and smile as God's new creation....

Become a Thankful Person
Pray this sample poem that might help you express your thanks to God:

I Am Yours, My God
O Love that flows within me always,
I am your special creation, new each day
in the refreshing springs of your love:
You speak to my womanspirit each day
love words that whole my soul and heal my heart.
—I love you.
—You are mine.
—You are my delight.
—I am loving through you.
Living Water, I praise you for the fountain of your love welling up within me, lifting me higher....
I am yours, my God, forever and ever.

A Psalm to Celebrate God's Spirit in Your Life
Pray this psalm or create your own to give voice to your celebration of the Holy Spirit's activity in your life:

God, your love dazzles me. Your divine energy
revitalizes my spirit.
New possibilities, fresh hopes, daring dreams
are emerging.
Your Spirit cherishes my creative power.
Sometimes I worry, become anxious,
and lose my way.
Cling to me in my times of struggle.
Your love melodies sing and dance within me,
all around me now and forever.
Blessed are you, God of my heart.

You understand me fully and love me totally
even when I don't know where I am going
or how I am getting there.
You show me the path to wisdom and fullness
of joy in your presence.
Gentle Spirit, your forgiveness delivers me from evil and
heals the wounds of sin in my soul,
free me from all misplaced priorities that I may
center my life on the fullness of your love.
God, you are my strength and peace,
the joy of my life.
You have poured out your Spirit on me.
May I see visions and dream dreams
as your prophets and saints of old.
Today I will expect a miracle.
I will soar on eagles' wings
as you lead me, O Promised Hope,
to show your compassion
to everyone and everything—aware that in you, we are all one.
Your life-giving Spirit appears in every face and
in every place.
May my heart be wide open to loving and
being loved.
Bless my hands this day that they may reach out
to touch tenderly the hurt in others' lives.
Bless my feet this day that they may travel the path to serve another
with kindness and generosity.
May your amazing grace overflow
in all my encounters.

*This chapter is adapted from *Praying With a Passionate Heart*
by Bridget Mary Meehan and Regina Madonna Oliver, 1999. Pp.49-
60 It is available from Online Retailers.

Chapter Thirteen:
Share With Soul Sisters

There is a feeling in the air now, a connection, an energy that is bringing women together from different generations, cultures, ethnic groups, and religions around the world. The global gathering of women that took place in Beijing in 1995 created ripples of hope for transformation for women in our society who dream of a new world in which there is peace and justice for people everywhere.

I experienced this same intuitive sense of women-power on *Godtalk*, a program that I produced and hosted for cable TV. In a series, "Women of Faith," women scholars from the Jewish, Muslim, and Christian traditions shared their perspectives on women in the Bible. As we dialogued, it became apparent that women from different backgrounds were exploring new pathways to healing and peace. We were able to relinquish our agendas and discover common ground. On one such program, a Muslim woman explained that Sarah, the Jewish matriarch, is revered in her tradition. The Jewish rabbi recalled the "bad rap" the Jewish rabbis who authored the midrash had given to Hagar. The African-American theologian discussed Hagar from the perspective of the black experience of oppression and empowerment. It occurred to me that here we were naming and confronting the biases that have kept religions apart for centuries. We were getting rid of misinformation and discussing new meanings that would enable these biblical women to mentor us in our spiritual journeys. We were discovering common ground. We were opening ourselves up to the Spirit in our midst.

Like the women scholars on *Godtalk,* women and men today can find spiritual enrichment in encountering biblical women such as Ruth and Naomi, Elizabeth and Mary, the Mother of Jesus, and Martha and Mary. These sisters of the faith can be role models for us as we strive to live the gospel in our times. Let us take a glimpse at a few of the stories of vibrant, human women who opened their hearts to other women as companions, friends, and soul sisters.

Ruth

In the Hebrew Scripture's Book of Ruth, we meet Ruth and her mother-in-law, Naomi. Ruth left her homeland in Moab and accompanied Naomi to Bethlehem after the deaths of Naomi's husband and sons. Upon her arrival, Ruth went to work, harvesting crops in the fields, to support Naomi. Here she met Boaz, a relative of Naomi. Naomi engaged in some clever matchmaking to bring Boaz and Ruth together. Ruth followed the advice of her mother-in-law, married Boaz, and gave birth to Obed, the grandfather of King David.

In this story, Ruth is praised for her faithful love and loyalty to Naomi. She refused to return to her homeland and vowed to follow Naomi wherever she went. Ruth proclaimed her deep affection for her mother-in-law: "Do not press me to leave you or to turn back from following you! Where you go, I will go; where you lodge, I will lodge; your people shall be my people, and your God my God. Where you die, I will die—there will I be buried" (Ruth 1:16–17 *New Revised Standard Version Bible*). There is no other example of friendship between human beings like Ruth's promise to Naomi anywhere else in the Bible. This is even more remarkable because Ruth was a foreigner, an outsider who left her family, religion, and culture to be a companion to Naomi. By taking this step, Ruth risked poverty, rejection, and ridicule. Yet, in a reversal, which scholars believe is a critique of Israel's ruling elite who excluded foreigners from their society, the biblical writers described Ruth as the heroine of the story.

Naomi was the ideal mother-in-law who looked out for Ruth's best interest. She guided Ruth into Boaz's embrace. According to the text, Naomi treated Ruth's baby like her own child. She nursed him, and her neighbors remarked that Ruth was of greater value to Naomi than seven sons—the ultimate compliment in this culture. How's that for gratitude!

Ruth and Naomi were two women who shared much of life's joy and sorrow. They were married, widowed, had children, and lived in exile in a foreign land. They helped each other. They had the kind of friendship that some women today experience and others seek. They were survivors in a society that marginalized them. Non-white women from different cultures, ethnic backgrounds, and religions today can relate to their survival skills. Like Ruth, God chooses the outsiders, the foreigners, or the marginalized in a society to be the models of God's inclusive love for all people everywhere. The story of Ruth and Naomi offers a powerful message that love can transform us and make a difference in our world. We do not need to allow our prejudices or biases to destroy us; rather, we can commit ourselves to lend a helping hand and a listening ear to those in need wherever we may find them. Sometimes, like Ruth and Naomi, we need look no further than our own families.

Mary and Elizabeth

According to the Gospel of Luke, Mary and Elizabeth were relatives and confidants who shared their innermost thoughts and feelings with each other. The angel appeared to Mary and announced her miraculous conception of Emmanuel, meaning "God with us," then told her the good news about Elizabeth: "And now, your relative Elizabeth in her old age has also conceived a son; and this is the sixth month for her who was said to be barren. For nothing will be impossible with God" (1:36–37 New Revised Standard Version Bible). As soon as Mary found out that Elizabeth was pregnant, she immediately dashed off to Elizabeth and Zachary's home for a three-month visit. I cannot help wondering if Mary had morning sickness when she undertook this arduous journey and if Elizabeth had a difficult pregnancy. One thing we know for sure is that they were both pregnant by divine intervention. Elizabeth was beyond menopause and had known infertility for many years. Mary, on the other hand, was young, fertile, but a virgin.

The moment Mary greeted her, Elizabeth's baby danced for joy in her womb. Filled with the Holy Spirit, Elizabeth affirmed Mary's motherhood. She recognized that her relative was carrying the body and blood of Christ within her. "Blessed are you among women, and blessed is the fruit of your womb. And why has this happened to me that the mother of my God comes to me? For as soon as I heard the sound of your greeting, the child in my womb leaped for joy" (1:42–44 *New Revised Standard Version Bible*).

Then Mary shared the depths of her gratitude with her wise mentor in the canticle of praise known as the Magnificat. Mary expressed in this prayer her profound experience of God's liberating love in her life and proclaimed the divine tender mercies that raise up the oppressed and poor and knock down the proud and arrogant.

This encounter between a young woman and an old woman, both pregnant reflects the hopes and dreams of women through the ages who are filled with the life-giving power of God. Christians today are challenged to be like Mary and Elizabeth, the Body of Christ birthing the life-giving power of God into the world. Like Mary, we can use our gifts to become companions to others in need; and, like Elizabeth, we can recognize and affirm the Christ within others around us and everywhere. Mary and Elizabeth are visible reminders that women can celebrate their identity because God continues to leap in wombs, touch hearts, and transform lives since God is in us and of us. Like Mary and Elizabeth, women today reflect the feminine face of God in our world.

As sure as Mary gave birth to God in human flesh, Christians can give birth to God over and over through acts of loving kindness to friends and strangers alike. All we have to do is embrace one another in genuine love, like our soul sisters Mary and Elizabeth. The Holy Spirit will do the rest, if we open our hearts, serve others, and sing God's praises.

Mary and Martha

No reflection on women's relationships in the Bible would be complete without a look at two of the most famous sisters in history—Mary and Martha. According to the story, Jesus is a guest in their home. Martha is busy preparing the meal, and Mary is relaxing in Jesus' presence, listening to his words. Right away, Martha bursts on the scene to complain about Mary's lack of helpfulness in preparing the meal: "Do you not care that my sister has left me to do all the work by myself? Tell her then to help me" (Luke 10:40 *New Revised Standard Version Bible*).

At first glance, Mary and Martha appear to be competitive sisters in conflict over their different agendas. Martha seems to be a nag who is at her wit's end with her sister's behavior, and Mary seems to be a bit withdrawn. But if we take another look, we see that Martha is a woman who gets things done. She is competent and unafraid to challenge her close friend, Jesus. According to the Gospel of John, Jesus loves Martha and reveals to her one of the most important messages in the history of Christianity — the meaning of the Resurrection. Martha's confession of Christ is similar to Peter's confession. According to the narrative, Jesus said to Martha, "I am the resurrection and the life. Those who believe in me, even though they die, will live, and everyone who lives and believes in me will never die. Do you believe this?" Martha replies, "Yes, Lord, I believe that you are the Messiah, the Son of God, the one coming into the world" (John 11:25–27 *New Revised Standard Version Bible*).

Now back to the supper scene. In his response to Martha's complaint about her sister, Jesus affirms women's value. In a society that placed little worth in women and viewed them as the property of men, Jesus asserts the rights of women to be disciples and equals with men. He affirms Mary as a learner and a disciple: "Martha, Martha, you are worried and distracted over many things, there is need of only one thing. Mary has chosen the better part, which will not be taken away from her" (Luke 10:41–42 *New* Revised Standard Version Bible).

When we feel envious or competitive with other women, perhaps we can find a clue to these drives in our driven "Martha-like" tendencies or our passive-aggressive "Mary side." Or, we could ask ourselves if we are adopting a male model of hierarchical values in our relationships with others. Elisabeth Schussler Fiorenza believes that Jesus' rebuke to Martha is a reflection of the patriarchal Church's attempt to keep women in a subordinate position (*In Memory of Her*, 165). Perhaps, as this renowned scholar suggests, Martha is a symbol of eucharistic ministry.

Today, contemporary women often face conflicts between their roles as caregivers and their roles as career professionals. Most women I know either feel guilty about their choice or exhaust themselves trying to do it all. Like Martha, we need to nurture the physical needs of our spouses, children, and older parents. Like

Mary, we need to care for all their spiritual needs. But like Martha, we need also to care for our own physical needs, and like Mary, we need to tend to our own spiritual hungers. The question often arises: *How can we be both Martha and Mary? Can we have it all, or do we need to choose?* There are no easy answers to these dilemmas. However, no matter what our choice, we can focus on the one necessary thing of which Jesus reminds us: We can live the liberating message of Jesus as disciples and equals. When we do this, we'll be able to affirm both the "Mary"| and "Martha"| in ourselves—no longer in competition but in harmony—showing us the way to wholeness and peace in our lives. We will be sisters and friends at last.

The stories of women in Scripture affect the way women think and feel about themselves. They remind us of our inner truths and struggles to live the gospel as faithful witnesses to Jesus' liberating presence in ambiguous times. They call us to live in solidarity with them as guides and soul mates—companions on the journey dwelling in God, working for justice and full of love for everyone and everything. What a treasure chest of womanspirit we have in our biblical sisters! Their witness energizes our hopes and dreams that the vision in the heart of Jesus—that all may be one—will become a reality in our times.

Prayer Experience: Share with Soul Sisters

Guided Prayer Encounter with Ruth and Naomi

Relax your body by releasing any stress you feel in your muscles. Start at the top of your head and proceed to the soles of your feet, alternately tightening and relaxing the muscles in each area of your body....Breathe deeply from the diaphragm....Feel the air as it moves in and out of your nostrils.... Imagine God breathing love, energy, peace, and joy into your body, mind, and spirit....Be aware that God is giving you whatever you most need right now.... Read the story of Ruth and Naomi in the Book of Ruth.... Conduct a mental conversation or write a letter to Ruth and/or Naomi, expressing your thoughts, insights, and feelings....

Invite Ruth and/or Naomi into your life for a day.... Let them accompany you through your activities, meet your family, friends....Sit down for a cup of tea or coffee and share with them your goals and challenges to live as a person of integrity and faith in our society....

Reflect on the marginalized, the outsiders, the foreigners, the people who are rejected or oppressed in our society....Ask Ruth and/or Naomi for ways you can reach out to them....

Share your close relationships with your biblical sisters....Name the gifts you have given and received from your women friends....

Choose one friendship to focus on now....Become aware of ways you experienced God's loving presence in your life through this special relationship.... Give thanks for this friend....Imagine Ruth and/or Naomi, your friend, and yourself in a circle of women, telling stories about faithful love and devoted friendship that nurture our womanspirits....

Be still and take this experience into the depths of your heart....Simply be with your close companions in God's Spirit....

Imagine a way to celebrate your close women relationships, such as sharing a meal, a phone call, a letter that expresses your appreciation for the gift of shared mutual love....

Encounter the Mary and Martha within You

In the stillness, open yourself to God's peace, harmony, joy, and love. If negative thoughts arise, simply let them float away as logs float down a river....

Repeat the words *peace, harmony, joy,* or *love* slowly....As you do so, image God's loving presence filling your mind, body, and spirit.... See yourself in a place of natural beauty....Let the Earth speak to you....Be attentive to flowers, plants, animals, trees, sky—all that you can see, hear, taste, touch, smell around you....Everywhere you turn, God is speaking to you about your connection with your environment....Write down your thoughts and feelings about the goodness of the Earth....

Reflect on God's acceptance of you as you are. Name your strengths and gifts...name your weaknesses and wounds...ask God to help you see yourself as God does....

Be aware of your "Mary" side (the contemplative/student) and your "Martha" side (the activist/achiever)....

Make a list of your gifts from each aspect of your personality. Write next to each what each gift has meant to you and to family, friends, neighbors, strangers, community, church, earth, world.

Reflect on ways you have developed your inner self and reached out in service in the last year....Be aware of the people who have encouraged your growth....Who are the people who have shaped your values? What struggles did you experience between your "Mary" and "Martha" sides, your contemplative and activist sides, your nurturing of self and others, your caregiving role and your career? What risks did you take? What connections did you make?

Be conscious of the Spirit's surprises that made you more aware of your need for balance and harmony in your life. How can you reconcile these two different dimensions of your personality? Write down your thoughts and feelings, insights, dreams about each of these encounters....

Be aware of opportunities for greater freedom and deeper love in your life. Are you willing to make the changes necessary for transformation to happen? for balance and harmony to occur? Write down your responses....

Be aware that God loves you in your imbalances and struggles...no one has it all together....

Imagine God embracing you with all your questions and shortcomings and ambiguities....Invite God to speak to your heart....Feel God's passionate love for you....Dialogue with God about the immeasurable depths of Divine Love for you as you are right now....

Play some of your favorite music. Paint, sculpt, sing, dance, or find some other way to celebrate your spiritual growth in the "Mary" and "Martha" aspects of your life....

Invite others to celebrate a time of growth, risk-taking, new beginning—a life-giving experience in the "Mary" and "Martha" dimensions of your personality....

Journal your thoughts and feelings about this sharing....

Guided Prayer Experience with Mary, the Mother of Jesus

Compose your own canticle of praise or Magnificat| for the gifts of God's loving tenderness in your life, or pray with Mary the following canticle:

My soul proclaims your goodness, O God,
and my spirit rejoices in you, my Savior.

For you have looked with favor
upon your lowly servant,
from this day forward
all generations will call me blessed.
For you, Holy One, have done great things for me,
and holy is your Name.
Your mercy reaches from age to age
for those who fear you.
You have shown strength with your arm,
you have scattered the proud in their conceit,
you have deposed the mighty from their thrones
and raised the lowly to high places.
You have filled the hungry with good things,
while you have sent the rich away empty.
You have come to the aid of Israel your servant,
mindful of your mercy —
the promise you made to our ancestors — to Sarah and Abraham
and their descendants forever
(Luke 1:46–55 *Inclusive New Testament*).

*This chapter is adapted from *Praying With a Passionate Heart* by Bridget Mary Meehan and Regina Madonna Oliver, 1999. Pp. 93-105. It is available from Online Retailers.

Chapter Fourteen:
Prayer Experiences for Loving from the Heart of God

T he following prayer experiences provide additional ways
you can discover a glimpse into God's love in your life.
These ways are meant to be savored and sampled as
delicious tastes‖ of divinity everywhere you turn.

The Prayer of Open Hands
Be still and quiet. Breathe in and out slowly.

In your imagination, be aware of the people you love...let
each one come to mind. Look into their eyes and share your
feelings of warmth and love with them...be aware of any areas
of concern you have...share these areas with them....

Open your hands and surrender your close relationships
one by one to God. Ask God to bless each person....

Be aware of any blockages in letting go and giving everyone
you love to God...be conscious of your feelings. Are you joyful?
anxious? sad? afraid? peaceful?

Share these feelings with God....

Express your appreciation for each relationship....

A Prayer of Gratitude for Life
Use the following as prayer starters, or compose your own
prayers of gratitude for life.

I thank you, God, for this day because....

I thank you, God, for tall trees that sway to the breath of
Divine Love in a gentle breeze....

I thank you, God, for sunny blue skies that radiate your shimmering, sparkling light....

I thank you, God, for furry creatures to caress and hold....

I thank you, God, for red and yellow tulips that grow in my spring garden....

I thank you, God, for snowflakes that cover the earth in a wholly white blanket on a winter's morn....

I thank you, God, for green grass that tickles my toes as I stroll on a summer's day....

I thank you, God, for the clear, cool water that refreshes my body and soul....

I thank you, God, for my family....

I thank you, God, for my friends....

I thank you, God, for my health....

I thank you, God, for my body and mind....

I thank you, God, for my faith....

I thank you for helping me to be a part of your plan for justice on earth.

A Prayer of Opening to Healing and Transformation
In this prayer, listen as God speaks healing words to your heart!

My love is like a wave breaking on the shore of eternity, forever washing over your weaknesses and wounds.

My mercy endures forever. Every time you fail, I will forgive and will heal you.

Alone you can do nothing. With me you can do everything.

Let my grace transform you and heal your heart.

Know that I make everything work together for the good of those who love me.

I can transform even your weaknesses and failures into blessings if you allow me.

Believe that you are filled with the healing presence of my Spirit.

Enter into my heart of divine compassion and let my love light a healing fire within your soul.

I release my power in your life now, and you will continue to grow in the depths and heights of my love.

Be at peace, my beloved. I am the God who dwells within you and embraces you **with tenderness forever.**

*This chapter is adapted from *Praying With a Passionate Heart* by Bridget Mary Meehan and Regina Madonna Oliver, 1999, 107-110. It is available from Online Retailers.

Chapter Fifteen:
A Bishop's Prayer for the Church

On April 19, 2009, the Roman Catholic Women Priests Movement celebrated our first ordinations of bishops in the United States on a beautiful sunny day in Santa Barbara, California. Bishops Patricia Fresen from Germany, Christine Mayr-Lumetzberger from Austria, and Ida Raming from Germany presided at this historic ordination of four women: Andrea Johnson, bishop of the Eastern Region, Joan Houk, bishop of the Great Waters Region, Regina Nicolosi, bishop of the Midwestern Region and myself, Bridget Mary Meehan, bishop of the Southern Region. A year later, Olivia Doko was ordained as bishop of the Western region

Janice Sevre-Duszynska, then our Southern Regional Administrator, presented me for ordination. She shared a touching testimony of the confidence that the women priests in our area had in me as nurturing companion, supportive sister, and therefore their choice as bishop. As I prostrated before the altar, I consecrated my life to God to work for the full equality of women in the church. As the assembly sang the melodic chant, invoking the Litany of the Saints to surround us, I knew that Mary, Mother of Jesus, Mary of Magdala, and St. Brigit of Kildare, bishop and abbess, were present along with my family and friends, both living and dead. I could picture my Mother smiling and sending support from heaven. A great cloud of witnesses, friends of God and prophets, both known to us and unknown, surrounded us and would help us as we set forth to walk on uncharted waters in our new ministry as bishops in a servant priesthood. Then, as the bishops and assembly laid hands on my head, I felt so much support from the people of God. It was a special joy that even though no one from my family could be physically present, they were represented by my dear friends, Bob and Peg Bowen, who held the Gospel Book over my head, Dorothy Irvin, who presented my Episcopal cross to the presiding bishop, and Lorraine Nagy, who presented my ring to the presiding bishop. Judy Johnson, Ruth Steinert Foote, and Marjorie Maquire came from across the country to attend, Rick Sapp, the director of GodTalk TV, filmed the ordination for the bishops and for YouTube. So, with them, and all the other Roman Catholic Women Priests who attended this celebration, we walked into history together again.

It has been over a year since my Episcopal ordination. In January, 2010, I had the honor of co-presiding at a festive liturgy dedicating the Housechurch of the Good Shepherd in Myers, Florida. Judy Lee serves the homeless and offers both physical aid and spiritual nurturance. The living room was packed with young and old and from different races and cultures. Several members of my community, Mary Mother of Jesus, drove 100 miles to participate with this Spirit-filled community. We blessed and dedicated this new worship space with heart-felt praise, thanksgiving, and sharing. Our sacred meal was followed by a hearty pot luck supper that nurtured our hearts and souls. Yes, as scripture reminds us that where God's people dwell as one, God is indeed present. Indeed, the homeless and those living on the margins often can teach us much about trusting in God's extravagant love.

A Bishop's Prayer for the Church
O Mothering God, Nurturer of Life,
Send forth your blessings on your creation.
Wisdom Sophia, enlighten us to see your
feminine face in women and men,
icons of your presence,
and in all beings.
May we live in harmony with

people of every race, religion and culture
Jesus, our love, free us and heal us.
Compassionate God,
Laugh with us on our merry way,
We stumble often, but you pick us up,
Dust us off and dry our tears.
We, your beloved, belong to you.
Spirit of Penecost, enflame our passion
to feed the hungers of humanity, physical, spiritual and
emotional.
May we, your people, reflect the goodness of others
back to them especially when they are discouraged or afraid.
Empower us with your Pentecost Fire
to speak truth to power, to work for justice and equality,
to help carry our neighbors' burdens
Partner, Companion, Friend, Love through us
Work through us
Comfort through us
Live in us
Dream with us
Help us believe
All things are possible in you, with you and through you as
miracles happen every day.

In your Heart, O God We are one, we are equal,
and we are loved. Forever and ever

God of justice and liberation,
Recreate us
As doers of justice
and advocates of peace
in a Christ-centered community
empowered by your Spirit
fostering the kindom of God
here and now
as we sing, dance, laugh
and celebrate your goodness in life.
Amen!

AFTERWORD:
Celebrating Inclusive Liturgies

M any Catholic Christians find themselves to be pilgrims in exile, walking a desert path as God is leading them out of misogynist and legalistic modes of worship and into the genuine worship of spirit and truth which does not revere power, but respects individuals as sacred and created in the image of God. As we struggle toward genuine expression of our ancient faith, we bring with us on the journey the mysterious and deep joy of knowing ourselves to be the Body of Christ in the continuance of the earthly pilgrimage.

In his book *The Future Of Eucharist,* Bernard Cooke observes that a new understanding of the resurrection in the Vatican II church has broadened the church's understanding of "real presence" and helped people to appreciate Christ's dynamic presence in the believing community. According to Cooke, while individuals may have specific functions within the gathered assembly, the entire community performs the Eucharistic action (p. 32). If this is so, then the gathered assembly *is* the celebrant of Eucharist. It is the community that "does" the Eucharist, not the Presider alone. A community encamps, wherever it happens to rest for this moment in time, around the Christ Presence that infuses our communion, vivifying our One Body.

Historical scholarship supports this conclusion and goes even farther. Gary Macy, chairperson of the Theology and Religious Studies Department at the University of San Diego, concludes

144

from his research that in Middle Ages manuscripts, regardless of who spoke the words of consecration - man or woman, ordained or community - the Christ presence became reality in the midst of the assembly. Contrary to the mindset of many contemporary Catholics who think that the way the Church is now was the way it was from the beginning, Dr. Macy observes that the theology of the Middle Ages was very broad in application. It was far less rigid than has usually been imagined and more open to different liturgical practices than we have realized. In other words, people were not declared heretics or thrown into prison for not following the norms (National Catholic Reporter. Jan. 9, 1998 p.5).

As we gather for the sacred meal, we celebrate a vision of faith, share joys and tears, acknowledge a cosmic citizenship as people of God, and model the equal ministry of women and men. We believe, as Paul did, that in the body of Christ there is no Jew, Greek, slave, citizen, male or female (Gal.3:20). All are welcome to celebrate Eucharist, not only families, but single parents and children, the divorced and remarried, gays and lesbians, married priests, women priests and all those who find themselves on the fringes of the institutional church for whatever reason. From my own experience of such community, we offer these prayers, which we hope will be helpful for other inclusive faith communities worshipping in the Catholic tradition.

The worship offered in these prayers of the gathered community reflects the tradition of the Church in that the Body of Christ gives the Body of Christ *to* the Body of Christ. As we remember, bless, and share the sacred meal, Christ becomes uniquely present among us, personally nourishing us in Eucharist. As we experience the presence of the Cosmic Christ in this sacrament, we become more aware that our lives are holy; our lives are blessed and broken in the mystery of God's transforming love. Christ continues to die and rise in our ordinary human experience. God's presence is always with us. Our Eucharistic Celebrations remind us that we are a community of believers called to be full of love as we bring peace and justice to the world.

We have a deep need to express, in action and words, the immense joy of this identity we share in Christ. We know that we participate in prayer rooted in the ancient tradition of Catholicism which, in turn, is rooted in a much more ancient tradition than itself. Joyfully we explore and are nurtured by those older ways as we continue to celebrate the rites familiar to us from our youth. We are part of the continuing dance of Creation with the Creator of the Universe, and we acknowledge the unfolding of this ever-new cosmic dynamism among us.

These liturgies were originally published by Woven Word Press in *Walking the Prophetic Journey*, co-authored by Mary Beben. This book is now out of print, so I have included my favorites. The last liturgy in this book is new: "Liturgy to Celebrate Justice, Partnership and Equality for Women in Church and Society." May these liturgies serve as a resource for spiritual growth for inclusive communities who worship in spirit and truth. The prayers and rituals can easily be adapted to the specific needs of any group. It is my hope that other pilgrims will experience the blazing fire of the Spirit's outpouring love as they enter into these celebrations of new life. As we take our place upon the cosmic altar of Creation, we fulfill Christ's high-priestly prayer that "all may be one," loving in the Heart of God

Liturgy for Advent/Christmas

Introduction of Theme:
Birther God comes to us this holy season through the stories of daring prophecies, shining stars, unforgettable dreams, singing angels, seeking magi, and the loving care of Mary and Joseph in a Bethlehem stable. As we contemplate the coming of Jesus long ago, let us birth Christ anew in our world today.

Opening Song:
Advent: "O Come, O Come Emmanuel,"or, "Prepare Ye the Way of the Lord," to melody from *Godspell*
Christmas: "O Come All Ye Faithful"

Greeting of Peace:
O Nurturing God, we celebrate your fruitful womb-love, as we embrace one another with joy.

Opening Prayer:
Birther God, you became human in Jesus and showed us how to live life fully. You know what it means to laugh and cry, to walk and talk, to love and be loved. There is nothing we could experience that you do not understand. We know that your mothering presence is always with us. May we, like Mary, rejoice as we give birth to God within us, and may we give birth to God in everything we say and do. Amen.

Readings:
(Suggestion: use *Inclusive Lectionary Texts* from *Priests for Equality*. Tel: 301-699-0042)
　　Zephaniah 3: 14-18 or Isaiah 25: 8-9 or Isaiah 40:1-2 or Isaiah 41: 17-18 or any of the Advent/Christmas Readings from the Hebrew scriptures 1 Thessalonians 5: 14-18, 2 Peter 3:8-14 or Galatians 4:4-7 or any reading from Advent/Christmas season
　　Gospel: Luke 1: 46-55 (Magnificat) or Luke 2: 16-21 (The birth of Jesus) or any gospel from Advent/Christmas season

Homily:

From the depths of God's womb love all of us are born. From the depths of God's womb love, Mary gave birth to Emmanuel, God-with-us. Mary, the first priest in our tradition, gave us the body and blood of Jesus. The Holy Spirit came upon her and the child she bore was God's Child. Jesus is born of a woman. Mary is the mother of God. Mother God is Mary's mother and our mother. God, the Birther of Life, nurtures us with divine womb-love from all eternity. During the Advent /Christmas season, we focus on the many ways we are birthers of God. We give birth to God within us and to God in everything, we say and do. We give birth to God every time we say a kind word, offer a helping hand, listen to a friend, visit the sick, and comfort the lonely.

When Katie and Danny were young children, they were "birthers" of God for me. They see new life bursting forth from mother earth everywhere. On our walks, they proclaimed God's glorious presence in small bugs, red berries, dandelions, tiny fish, birds, squirrels, wiggly worms, sparkling waters, and billowy clouds. When I was with them, a tremendous energy for play was born within me. They have shown me how to experience God's delight in my life in a whole new way by looking at everything with awe-filled eyes and by recognizing the grace-laden moments of ordinary life. Christmas, for me, is becoming a year-round celebration of God's birthing new gifts and treasures in my life to share with others. All I have to do is be open and let it happen as Mary did, and as Katie and Danny have shown me.

Today we are called to give birth to a new form of Eucharistic worship in our church. We are discovering that, as the body of Christ, we "make" Eucharist happen. Perhaps it is time to ask ourselves: "Do we believe that Birther God is becoming incarnate today in the believing community in powerful ways?" Let us reflect on some of our miraculous God-birthings.

Shared Dialogue:

The community shares their thoughts on the theme.

Intercessions:

For a deeper coming of Christ in our world, let us pray... (Response is: Birther God, hear us.)

That we may experience the birthing of God anew in our lives, we pray...

That people who suffer from destitution and despair may experience the mothering comfort of God in their lives, we pray...

That the sick and suffering (especially mention specific names) may receive the nurturing, healing love of God, we pray...

That those who have died (especially mention specific names) may rest in God's eternal womb, we pray...

(Other Intentions)

Presentation of the Bread and Wine:

(Hold up bread and wine) Blessed are you, God of all life, through your goodness we have bread, wine, all creation, and our own lives to *offer*. Through this sacred meal may we become your new creation.

The Eucharistic Prayer:

Part One:

Birther God, you brought forth all creation from your Life-Giving Womb. O Love of the Ages, who was born from Mary's womb, we praise you and leap for joy in your presence.

O Holy One of ancient Israel, you revealed yourself in Mary's womb, in a shining star, in humble shepherds, in a baby wrapped in swaddling clothes. You embrace us with infinite love in every situation and relationship. You dwell in the depths of our hearts.

We invite you this day to set us free, heal us, transform us and empower us as we gather around the table of your love. As we celebrate this sacred mystery in the embrace of the Holy One of birthing, we proclaim your praise:

All: Holy, Holy, Holy, Birther of heaven and earth. All beings are pregnant with your glory. Hosanna in the Highest. Blessed are you who dwell in all things. Hosanna in the Highest.

Part Two:

Praise to you, all-giving God, born of Mary. You are the body and blood of woman. We glorify you, nurturing God for the dawning of the sacred promise of God's Anointed, fulfilled in Jesus, the Christ.

We celebrate the birth of Jesus, our newborn Emmanuel who came to give us fullness of life. During this holy season we share the bread of freedom and lift the cup of salvation. We invite all, especially those on the fringe of church and society, to join us around this banquet of love.

As Jesus gave birth to the New Covenant, he took bread, gave thanks, broke the bread, and shared it with all those present saying:
All: Take this all of you and eat it. This is my body which will be given up for you.

At the end of the meal Jesus took a cup of wine, blessed you, Birther of Life, shared the cup with all those present saying:
All: Take this all of you and drink from it; this is the cup of my blood, the blood of the new and everlasting covenant; it will be shed for you and for all.

Let us proclaim the sacred presence of our nurturing God:
All: Christ, by your laboring on the cross, and your rising to new life, you have given birth to the new creation.

Part Three:

As we wait with joyful hearts for the fulfillment of your birthing power in our lives, we remember the prophets, martyrs, saints and mystics who have gone before us: Deborah, Isaiah, Mary of Magdala, Peter, Martha, Phoebe, Lydia, Irene, Patrick, Brigit of Kildare, Francis of Assisi, Hildegarde of Bingen, Catherine of Siena, Ignatius Loyola, Teresa of Avila, John of the Cross and all those we remember as heros and heroines in our church who inspire us today (Community names, mentors whom they want to remember, living and dead. This list is only partial. Each community needs to create their own according to custom and culture.)

Open us to the inbreaking of your healing love in every area of our lives creating within us new life. When we feel sorrow, give your comfort. When we are empty, fill us with your fullness. When we are confused, guide us with your wisdom. when we are lost, search for us and bring us home.

Part Four:

Embrace us in our brokenness and help us prepare in love for Christ's birth in our lives. Impregnate the people of God with the power of Spirit-Church. May your Spirit birth a new world of peace and justice. May everyone feel accepted and welcome in our community.

Nurture our families and friends with love and peace (especially those we pray for at this time) Embrace the sick and those who have died (name specific people in need of prayer) in your motherly arms.

May we give birth to the Word Made Flesh in us everyday of our lives. May we give birth to the church of our dreams and hopes. May we give birth to a deep reverence for earth and live in harmony with all creatures in the earth of the new creation.

All: Through Christ, with Christ, in Christ, all praise and glory are yours, Birther God, through the power of the Holy Spirit. Amen.

The Prayer of Jesus: (Traditional or see appendix)

Breaking of Bread:
Let us share the Body of Christ with the Body of Christ! Amen.

Communion:
Sing a favorite Advent or Christmas song such as "Silent Night" or "Away in the Manger" etc.

Prayer after Communion:
Birther of Life, Breast of Compassion, thank you for nourishing us in your sacrament. Make your presence continue to bring birth to your faithful people, through Emmanuel, God-with-us. Amen.

Final Blessing of Community:
May our mothering God bring us to birth in every area of our living. May Emmanuel, God-with-us, fill us with radiant joy. May we be birthers of hope in our world, and may God bless us always with divine strength to walk justly and serve generously all those we encounter. Amen.

Closing Song:
Advent: "O Come, O Come Emmanuel" or "Prepare Ye the Way of the Lord" from *Godspell*
Christmas: "Joy to the World"

Liturgy of Water

Introduction of Theme:
You are a very special vessel that God has prepared in your own special way to be a gift to all of us! Let us sing our opening hymn as an offering of those gifts back to God.

Opening Song:
"Come To The Water" by the St. Louis Jesuits

Greeting of Peace:
Peaceful Waters, we share the abundant love that flows among us as we embrace each other with open hearts.

Opening Prayer:
Spirit of God, you moved over the waters breathing life, freedom and joy into creation. Fill us, bathe us, drench us with your healing, refreshing love. Make us a life-giving river spilling over and splashing justice, truth and love over all.

Blessing of the Water:
May this water be blessed by Mother Earth who has given it to us, by Father Sky who has rained it down upon us, and by the Spirit of the Living God, whose nature it represents.

Blessing of the People:
May you be blessed and renewed in your baptismal promises to God, yourself, and the People of God! (Sprinkle all, including presider, with blessed water.)

Readings:
Matthew 3:13-17 or John 5:42f or Genesis 1:1-2

Homily:
Create atmosphere by placing a bowl of water or a picture of the ocean, a waterfall, etc., in the background. Begin sharing time by singing a simple centering hymn such as "Waterfall" By Cris

Williamson - *Bird Ankles Music* or "Spirit of the Living God, Fall Afresh On Us."

Homilist leads group in five minutes of silence in which community is invited to experience the Living Water in whatever images, insights, thoughts or feelings emerge. Play some instrumental music or sounds of ocean in background. Invite participants to relax, close their eyes, breathe deeply, and be present to the Living Water. Then invite participants to share a story, incident, example or image from their prayer that has touched them.

If the theme is on baptism, focus the discussion on the meaning of baptism or the call to live the gospel in our everyday life. You could begin with open-ended statements, such as: I believe God is calling me to... I believe I am beloved of God because... My greatest challenge in living as a Christian today is... Baptism means... When my child/grandchild was baptized, I felt... I understood... I experienced....

Shared Dialogue:
The community shares their thoughts on the theme.

Intercessions:
That we may be faithful to our promises to the People of God, we pray... (Response is: "Hear us, O God!")

That we may use earth's resources wisely, we pray...

That the Spirit of God, like Living Water, would break down resistances and barriers between people and between groups of believers, we pray...

(Other intentions)

Presentation of the Bread and Wine:
(Hold up bread and wine) Blessed are you, God of all life, through your goodness we have bread, wine, all creation, and our own lives to offer. Through this sacred meal may we become your new creation.

The Eucharistic Prayer:
Part One:
We praise you, Wellspring of Love, in whom we live and move and have our being. You have sent Jesus, Sophia's child, the Wisdom of

the Ages, to show us that the heart of religion is worshipping you in spirit and in truth. You revealed your identity to the Samaritan woman at the well. You continue to reveal your identity to us today. You embrace every nation, race, creed and culture as your own.

O Divine Companion, you look at each of us with great tenderness. May we see ourselves loved by you totally. (Invite people to touch with reverence their own faces and say softly to themselves a prayer like: "I am the compassionate face of God" or "God's Spirit dwells within me.")

God of relationships, you reveal yourself in other people. (Invite people to look with love at the faces in the gathered assembly for a moment or two.) Holy One, Compassionate One, Gracious One, your glory embraces heaven and earth. Like sun-drenched waters that sparkle, all human faces reflect your radiant splendor. You love each of us as if we were the only person in the world. Blessed is Jesus who comes in the name of Sophia! Hosanna in the highest.

Part Two:
O surging Ocean of Grace, you energize us with Spirit and passion, connecting us with all creatures in the depth of your unending love. You wash us clean of resentment and hostility and scrub away the debris that pollutes our spirits. We ask you to make us new as you did in the waters of our baptism. Immerse us in the Love that dances for joy in your presence. We gather to celebrate our sacred stories as we welcome all people around this banquet table. We remember Jesus-Sophia who invites us to come and drink of the waters that will quench our thirst forever.

The night before pouring forth his love for all people, Jesus took bread, broke it and shared it with his beloved companions, saying:
All: Take this, all of you, and eat it. This is my body which will be given for your healing.

Then, looking with tender warmth on his friends, Jesus took a cup of wine, praised Sophia, and shared the cup, saying:
All: Take this all of you and drink from it; this is the cup of my blood, the blood that will satisfy the longings of human hearts for all times. It will be poured out for the healing and wholeness of all creation. Remember always you are a reflection of divinity.

Part Three:

Let us proclaim the mystery of our dying and rising in Christ: Jesus-Sophia comforts us in our losses, cries with us in our sorrow, and promises that our innermost beings will flow with rivers of living water, even in the midst of our suffering and pain.

As we share this holy meal, we remember the holy men and women who drank from Wisdom's well and showed us how to live as courageous disciples: the prophet Miriam, King Solomon, the woman at the well, Paul of Tarsus, Prisca and Aquila, Clare and Francis of Assisi, Dorothy Day, Jean Donovan, Dorothy Kazel, Ita Ford, Maura Clark, Oscar Romero and all those companions we cherish and who bless and challenge us on our faith journey.

Part Four:

May the Church be anchored in the still waters of your presence where abundant blessings flow forever. 0 Holy One who lives in our hearts, we celebrate your radiant image in men and women everywhere. Your creativity flows through our beings. Your joy fills us. Your blessings are the wellspring of grace all around us. Your mercy is fresh, like dew, every morning. Your healing liberates us from all darkness and oppression. Your empowerment bubbles up inside us. For you are the Love that dwells in our depths, the Wisdom of the Ages that speaks through us, the Divine Connection that makes us all one. Amen.

The Prayer of Jesus: (Traditional or see appendix)

Breaking of Bread:
Let us share the Body of Christ with the Body of Christ! Amen.

Communion:
"Let Justice Roll Like A River" - *Gather Comprehensive* - G.I.A. Hymnal or "Healing River" by F. Hellerman and Fran Miakoff, sung by Pete Seeger on *I Can See A New Day*

Prayer After Communion:

O God, thank you for refreshing us in your sacrament. May we experience your life-giving waters welling up within us as we serve others with glad hearts. Amen.

Final Blessing of Community:

May the Spirit who moved over the waters of creation renew the earth. May Jesus Sophia satisfy our thirst for living fully. May the God of play fill our hearts to overflowing this day with our hearts' delights.

Closing Hymn:

"Healing River" by Peter Seeger or "Washerwoman God" (Lyrics by Martha Ann Kirk; sung by Colleen Fulmer on *"Cry of Ramah"* - Loretto Spirituality Network, 725 Calhoun St., Albany,CA 94706. Tel: 510-525-4174.

Liturgy of Light
(Appropriate during Lent, Ordinary Time, and special occasions)

Introduction of Theme:

Have a circle of candles in the center of the worship space for each person in the assembly. Invite participants to light a candle and say a prayer that expresses how they are reflections of God's love in the world, e.g. I am a radiant reflection of divine goodness... I am a community- builder... I am a person of peace... I reflect kindness and/or patience when I _____, etc. Or the focus could be on how the community/church/earth/world is light.

Radiant Light, you surround us, heal us, shine through us, and energize us. Brilliant Brightness, illuminate the cosmos that we may see your beauty, goodness and love everywhere. Like Jesus, we are the light of the world reflecting divinity's splendor.

Opening Song:

"City of God," by the St. Louis Jesuits or "This Little Light of Mine" or "Sing A Blessing" by Miriam Therese Winter from *Woman Prayer/Woman Song* - Medical Mission Sisters

Greeting of Peace:

Let us share the Living Light dwelling in our hearts with one another.

Opening Prayer:

Enlightener of the Ages, your belief in us far surpasses our belief in ourselves. May we see ourselves more clearly as you see us. May we hope always in the Love that is always more than enough. May we act courageously, conscious that we can do all things because of your power within us. Like you, may we let our light shine everywhere. Amen.

Readings:

Lent: 1 Samuel 16:1,6-7,10-13; Ephesians 5:8-14; Isaiah 2:4-5
Ord. Time: Jeremiah1:4-5, 17-19; 1 Corinthians 12;31-13:13 1 John 1:5-7 Gospel: Lent : John 9: 1-41; Ordinary Time: Luke 4:16-30, Special Occasion: Luke 8:16

Homily:

Today's readings focus on Jesus as the light of the world. Like Jesus, we are living lights of God's presence in the world producing goodness and justice. The Enlightener of the Ages sees us as we really are - gifts and wounds - and believes that we can do marvelous things. The Holy One has a vision for our life that far surpasses our wildest hopes or dreams. Each of us is a brilliant reflection of God. But so often we are not conscious of our amazing potential.

Let us take a few minutes to reflect on who we really are! (Use instrumental music in the background) Begin by relaxing, breathing deeply, and gazing at the circle of candles. Focus on one candle. Close your eyes and journey to the depths of your being. See yourself as you are before God. Become aware that God believes in you more than you have ever imagined. Listen to God speak in the silence of your heart. See yourself in the light of God's hopes and dreams for your life. You are radiant... loved.... free.... at peace with others... one with creation. See yourself as a living light of God's love, shining brilliantly. Be aware of your thoughts, feelings, any images, insights, or questions that arise. Slowly and gently, open your eyes and come back to the circle of candles. Take time to share anything you want from your reflection, any insights you have from the readings or your answers to the following questions:

How are you a living light of God? Name others who are living lights of God for you.

How is this community, the church, Earth, the Cosmos, a light of God?

Shared Dialogue:

The community shares their thoughts on the theme.

Intercessions:

That we may care for the cosmos in which the Holy One is revealed, we pray to you our Creator...

(Response is Hear us, O God!)

That theologians may have courage to respond to the rhythm of truth in spite of condemnation, we pray to you, our Creator...

That we may persevere in working for the fullness of justice in our world, we pray to you, our Creator...

That the sick may be healed, especially (mention names), we pray to you, our Creator...

(Other Intentions...)

Presentation of the Bread and Wine:

(Hold up bread and wine) Blessed are you, God of all life, through your goodness we have bread, wine, all creation, and our own lives to offer. Through this sacred meal may we become your new creation.

The Eucharistic Prayer:

Part One:

God of Light, you shine everywhere in our universe, warming all creatures with your bright rays. God of the stars, you write our names in the velvety darkness of night. God of sun and moon, you reveal the magnificence of creation all around us. Flowers and trees, mountains and oceans, birds and bugs and all our favorite creatures reflect your glory night and day. We praise you for your brilliance, enlightening our minds and guiding us with insight to make decisions and choose paths that lead to fuller freedom.

Risen Christ, you lead us out of the darkness of sin into the glory of eternal life as we glimpse your infinite love alive in us. How wondrous are your works, too numerous to name! The splendor of your unending light sparkles forever in our hearts. We sing your praises as we say:

All: Holy, Holy, Holy, heaven and earth are covered with your glory. Hallelujah for all that has been, is now, and will be. Blessed is the One who is always faithful.

Part Two:

We glorify you, Source of Brightness, for illuminating the cosmos with your indwelling presence. We praise you for the beautiful colors of the rainbow painted across the sky as a sign of your faithfulness. We thank you for sending Jesus, the Light of the World, to shine in our darkness and to show us the way to live in peace and justice with all people.

We remember Jesus, who came to illuminate the shadows of our inner world and to shine the light of truth on the darkness of our outer world. The Light of the Ages challenged us to reach out to another, offer forgiveness to the person who rejects us, free the oppressed and stand in solidarity with the outcasts of society. Jesus calls us to love one another with tender compassion and mercy. We ask now that the power of divine goodness move through our beings and transform us to be channels of healing to the people who come into our lives - our families, friends, co-workers, neighbors, even our enemies. So, Healing Light, shine upon us once again as we recall the banquet of your self-giving love. We consecrate ourselves to you, giving ourselves totally to you in mind, body and spirit. Pour out your Spirit upon us and make us whole.

Part Three:
The night before Jesus gave up his life for us, he took bread, broke it and shared it with the friends he cherished saying,
All: Take this all of you and eat it; this is my body which will given for you, as a sign of the love I have for you from the dawning of eternity.

Then Jesus took a cup of wine, praised Shekinah, the Light of the heavens that guided the Hebrew people in the desert, and shared the cup saying,
All: Take this all of you and drink from it; this is the cup of my blood, the blood that will nurture your soul; it will be poured out for your liberation. Do this in my memory.

Let us rejoice as we remember that we are the body and the blood of the Risen Christ. God of Light, kindle the fire of your love in our hearts. Enable us to act justly, love tenderly, and walk humbly with you. Risen Sun, you have died that we may no longer be blind. You have risen that we may see with the eyes of faith and you will come again every day to shine hope into the darkness of negativity and sin around us. May our lives glow with goodness as a candle shines in the darkness. May the leaders of our world and church, and all those who suffer from hunger, poverty, and discrimination walk in your radiant splendor. May all who have died rest in your eternal light.

Part Four:
May the saintly women and men of old, the cloud of witnesses who have gone before us, accompany us on our journey. They are our

soul friends with whom we bond and whom we cherish. Let us pause now to name these people who have been an inspiration to us. May their courage, faith and determination be bright beacons of hope and encouragement to us.

Radiate in our hearts, God of exuberance; blessed are we who are one with you. May we reflect your holy presence and lifegiving power as we carry each other out of the darkness of misunderstanding, hatred, and fear into the wondrous light of understanding, love and trust.

Make us your co-workers in affirming human dignity. Help us to challenge a culture that seeks to dominate rather than to empower. May we be prophetic in working for systemic justice, always questioning structures that oppress, denigrate, and exclude women, homosexuals, foreigners, and all the contemporary outcasts in our society today. As the prophet Isaiah said, when we speak truth to power, our wound will be quickly healed. Consecrate us now in your truth as we pray for a new outpouring of the Spirit in our time:

All: Through Christ, the Light of the World, with Christ, the Light of the World, in Christ, the Light of the World, all glory, power and honor is yours Creator of the Universe, through the power of the Spirit that makes us all one now and ever. Amen.

(Place candles on table and join hands.)

The Prayer of Jesus: (Traditional or see appendix)

Breaking of Bread:
(Hold up bread and wine) Through this sacred meal may we become your new creation. Let us share the Body of Christ with the Body of Christ!

Communion:
Instrumental Music - Mike Rowland's "The Fairy Ring" or any song from John Michael Talbot's *The God of Life.* or "Jesus, Wonderful Counselor" (*Praise Six* by the Maranatha Singers)

Prayer after Communion:
Thank you, God, for the meal we have shared in your memory. May we go forth from here as a light of your love, more deeply aware of

our communion with God and all creatures. Through the power of your Spirit, we pray. Amen.

Final Blessing of Community:
May the love of God enfold us; may the light of God brighten our paths; may the Spirit of God dance within our hearts as we go from glory to glory on our pilgrimage to eternity's shore.

Closing Song:
"Come to the Circle" by Kathy Sherman in *Once Upon a Universe* published by Sisters of St. Joseph, La Grange, Illinois 1-800-354-3504. or " Send us Forth, 0 Christ Sophia" by Jann Aldredge-Clanton, published by Twenty-Third Publications, 1-800-321-0411.

Liturgy on The Cosmic Dance
(Spring or Summer)

Introduction of Theme:

Our Creator calls us to join the cosmic dance of creation - women, men, children, all creatures - leaping, spinning, twirling through time and space in a celebration of praise that echoes throughout the universe forever. Let us put on our dancing shoes and feel the divine energy of Spirit-Life moving among us, around us, within us - everywhere we turn.

Opening Song:

"Circle of Love" by Miriam Therese Winter

Greeting of Peace:

(Music: Instrumental music. Group forms a circle and move three steps to the right and then one step to the left as the music plays. Other steps could be designed by liturgical planners in response to the culture and creativity of the community.)

Let us join hands in a circle and move to the right and to the left at the beat of the music. As we do so, let us experience the energy of the divine dance connecting us in love with all creation. Let our circle dance express our deep desire for peace and harmony in the cosmos.

(Alternate Greeting:) Let us join hands in a circle as a sign of our solidarity with all creation.

Opening Prayer:

In the name of our God who dwells within us, in the name of our God, who is bearer of earth's magnificent gifts: daffodils and oak trees, sparkling oceans, and majestic mountains, strong bears and tiny kittens, in the name of our God who dances on moon beams, and leaps for joy across the heavens, let us give thanks and praise.

Readings: Genesis 1:1-27; Gospel: John 14:11-21

Homily:

As we listen to the affirmation of the Creator, proclaiming the creation to be good in the Genesis story of creation, we receive a divine invitation to dance forever with the Divine Mystery that is sometimes hidden, sometimes unveiled in everyone and everything we encounter.

My niece Katie and nephew Danny have shown me how glorious is dancing with the Holy One. Sometimes it means putting on shoes and jumping in puddles, or dining with princes and princesses, or running barefoot through the grass, or imitating mother eagle teaching her baby eaglets how to fly, or playing and splashing in a swimming pool on a warm summer's day.

In the Gospel of John, Jesus shows the way to fullness of life, telling us that anyone who has faith in him will do the works he did - and greater works besides. The Risen One continues the dance of divine creativity in us who journey together, sisters and brothers with all living things on the way to the new creation where heaven and earth will be completely one - new and glorious with Spirit Creator as it was in the beginning, is in the process now, and will be forever to endless ages. We glimpse this vision, as in a glass darkly even now, as we strive to live in harmony with God's creation affirming, as God did at the birth of creation, that all things are good.

Jesus challenged us to greater works in the gospel. At the dawning of the 21st century, we are at the brink of undreamed-of possibilities to explore other planets and probe the new visions of the Mystery of Life. What does all this mean? Does it involve a fresh understanding of matter, energy, spirit and life? Are we called to be prophets and mystics? Now, more than ever it is time to put on our dancing shoes!

Shared Dialogue:
The community shares their thoughts on the theme.

Intercessions:
Let us dance together the dance of becoming with God. That we may care for the cosmos in which the Holy One is revealed, we pray to you our Creator... (Response is: Lead us, O God!)

That those in leadership in our church may let go of fear of the new and wholeheartedly join in the dance, we pray to you, our Creator...

That theologians may have courage to respond to the rhythm of truth in spite of condemnation, we pray to you, our Creator...

That the dead may dance forever in God's presence, we pray...

(Other Intentions)

Presentation of Bread and Wine:

(Hold up bread and wine) Blessed are you, God of all life, through your goodness we have bread, wine, all creation, and our own lives to offer. Through this sacred meal may we become your new creation.

Eucharistic Prayer:

Part One:

God of amazing surprises, Creator of tiny bugs and awesome planets, Designer of earth's wonders, Giver of life and laughter, we praise your passionate love hidden, yet revealed, everywhere in the cosmos.

We thank you that from the beginning, you called us to partnership with all creation in the holy dance that is all of life in your Divine Presence. We praise you as we jump for joy in an explosion of grace that resounds through the universe.

All: Holy, Holy, Holy, God of dance and song, heaven and earth are robed in your glory. Hosanna in the Highest. Blessed are You who dwell among us. Happy are we who are called to this banquet of unending joy. Hosanna in the Highest.

Part Two:

We thank you for the women and men through the ages who have danced Love's cosmic dream of communion with hearts ablaze. We pause now to remember those who have shown us how to step lightly on the path to holiness. (Time for spontaneous remembrance)

We praise you, Christ, who calls us to deep intimacy in this Eucharistic celebration. We offer thanks for this gift, the Bread of Life and the Cup of Salvation, that will heal our hearts and transform our lives.

Part Three:

Before Jesus freely gave his life for us, he took bread, gave thanks, broke the bread, gave it to his friends and said:

All: Take this all of you, and eat it. This is my body which will be given up for you.

At the end of the meal, Jesus took a cup of wine, gave you thanks and praise, gave the cup to his friends and said:

All: Take this, all of you, and drink from it. This is the cup of my blood, the blood of the new and everlasting covenant. It will be shed for you and for all so that creation may reconciled. Every time you do this, remember me.

Let us proclaim the mystery of faith:

Christ, in your dying and rising, all creation leaps together toward a new earth and new heavens. Although we come from diverse backgrounds, we are one body, for we all share in this one bread. And so, as we join with one another in the cosmic dance, Creator God, we celebrate your holy presence in every living thing.

Let us live as a new body, brought to birth by the Spirit of the Risen One in acts of forgiveness, healing, and justice. Let us support all who suffer and work for peace in lands torn by violence and hatred.

All: Through Christ, with Christ, in Christ, in the resurrecting power of Divine Love, all glory and praise is yours, O Gracious God, forever.

The Prayer of Jesus: (Traditional or see appendix)

Breaking of Bread:
(Hold up bread and wine) Let us share the Body of Christ with the Body of Christ!

Communion:
Meditation Hymn: "In the Name of God" from John Michael Talbot's cassette "*The God of Life*"

Prayer after Communion:
Cosmic Christ, you have lifted us up and swung us around to see your beauty in nature's awesome gifts everywhere and in everyone. May we continue to move together to the divine rhythm of harmony and peace, dancing joyfully in love with all created beings forever.

Final Blessing of Community:
May we go forth as dancing prophets and mystic visionaries of our cosmic communion with all life, in the Name of the Creator, in the Name of the Healer, in the name of the Spirit. Amen

Closing Song:

"Come To The Circle Of Life" by Kathy Sherman on *"Faces of The Children"* or "Dancing Sophia's Circle" by Colleen Fulmer from cassette *"Dancing Sophia's Circle"*- Loretto Spirituality Network, 725 Calhoun St., Albany, CA *94756* Tel: 510-525-4174.

Liturgy of Fire
(Easter Season, Pentecost, Earth Day, Social Justice)

Introduction of Theme:
O Holy One of burning bushes, enflame us with your passion for life, for justice, for creativity, for renewal, for play. Shekinah, appearing in the symbols of cloud, light and fire, you accompanied the Hebrew people through the wilderness. Travel with us through our desert and lend us a glimpse of your powerful feminine presence among us. Divine Compassionate Love, be our source of strength in our commitment to justice and peace. Dwell within us always as an eternal flame that will glow forever.

Opening Song:
"We're Coming Home" by Carolyn McDade or "You, God, are my Firmament" by Miriam Therese Winter, published by Medical Mission Sisters, or "Come Thou From Whom All Blessings Flow" by Jann Aldredge-Clanton, published by Twenty-Third Publications 800-321-0411 or "Come Holy Spirit" or "Veni Sancte Spiritus" from Taize on *Laudate* tape.

Greeting of Peace:
Let us reach out in love to one another.

Opening Prayer:
Shekinah, you show us the sacredness of Earth and all her creatures. You reveal yourself in wind, fire, and earth. May we celebrate with burning hearts the warmth of your passionate love in the outpouring of your miracles everywhere. May we join with others in works of justice and peace for our world.

Readings:
Pentecost: Joel 3:1-5, Romans 8:22-27
Women at Pentecost: Acts 1:12-14 or Acts 2:1-18 Shekinah: Exodus 29:45-46 or Exodus 25:8
Gospel: John 7:37-39, Matthew 9:17, Luke 1:46-56 or Luke 24:13-35

Homily:

Where is the passion in your life? Is the Pentecost-Fire stirring in you?

Has Shekinah whispered anything in your ear lately? What makes your heart bum within you?

I see and hear the Spirit "a'movin'" all over the place. I glimpse her presence in the feminine awakening in which women from different religions and traditions are voicing their truth, claiming their inner authority, turning away from patriarchal values and embracing their spiritual experiences.

Another place I discover her impact is in the re-emergence of feminine divine imagery in creative rituals and traditional worship. As I use these images in my prayer, I am discovering a new dimension of myself. For the first time in my life I see myself as a powerful reflection of God's feminine face. Gender equality is now more than a head trip for me. It is at the heart of the transformation of patriarchy. It is the vision of Jesus and it will change everything.

The scripture readings speak to us of Spirit-Fire spreading through the cosmos, recreating Earth, renewing human hearts and transforming the church. The same Spirit-Fire nudges people of our age to dream new dreams of a world where there is no more discrimination, and inspires visions of justice, equality and peace. Shekinah continues her whisperings through contemporary prophets, like Dorothy Day who, with her vision of nonviolence and pacifism, shakes people up. Indeed, Shekinah seems to be doing a lot of shaking up today. Many structures and institutions seem to be falling apart.

Excitement, fear, doubt and confusion abound. A paradigm shift appears on the horizon. Where are you? Is the Spirit an ill wind shaking you up or like a gentle mother comforting you? Or both? Is Shekinah guiding you over the rugged mountains and low valleys of your struggles with life's ambiguities? Where are we as a faith community in our journey toward the fullness of justice? Will the church be renewed? It looks like we are back where we started, full of questions, full of wonder at Spirit Presence dwelling among us. Let's take some time to share the "miracles" of Pentecost-Fire, the whispering of Shekinah in your life.

Shared Dialogue:
The community shares their thoughts on the theme.

Intercessions:
Let us pray that Spirit-Fire may light up our world and renew all hearts. (Response is: Yes, Shekinah!)

That we may realize that creation is Shekinah's sanctuary, we pray...

That each of us may experience ourselves as Shelcinah's dwelling place, we pray...

That the Spirit may transform all unjust structures in church and society, we pray...

(Other Intentions)

Presentation of Bread and Wine:
(Hold up bread and wine) Blessed are you, God of all life, through your goodness we have bread, wine, all creation, and our own lives to offer. Through this sacred meal may we become your new creation.

The Eucharistic Prayer:
Part One:
O Divine Flame of Love, your glowing embers dance in our hearts. Your passionate presence kindles our souls. You purify us with the searing truth that ignites our spirits. As the glowing embers of a fire penetrate the cold around us, so your tenderness sets our hearts aglow. We celebrate your nearness this day as we remember your Pentecost miracles.

How often have you loved us tenderly, without limits or boundaries! How often have you forgiven us freely and healed our sicknesses! How often have we been consumed with delight by human touch!

How often have you embraced us through Earth's beauty! How often have you affirmed us as your beloved creation! How often have you energized us to keep on keeping on - working for justice and peace in our world! We praise and exalt you forever with grateful hearts as we pray:

All: Holy, Holy, Holy, Fire of Love, heaven and earth burn with love for you. Blessed are you who come to show us the depths of your yearning for us. Hosanna in the highest.

Part Two:
Passionate God, kindle your fire of enthusiasm within us. Speak to us with assurance and excitement. Reveal to us the infinite, boundless, depths of your love for us. Awaken us to your promises to be always present in our lives, no matter what the obstacles or setbacks we experience. Consume us with such a hunger and thirst for justice that our words and actions may inflame others to become signs of your justice. Give us eyes to see human need, hearts to care for our sisters and brothers and hands and feet to lighten others' burdens.

Part Three:
Shekinah, we thank you for sending Jesus, your strong, but gentle presence, to bless and transform our lives. Jesus came to pour forth the love from your heart on all of us and show us how to live as your new creation.

The night before Jesus died, he gave us a special gift of love divine. He took bread, broke it and shared it with friends who gathered around the table saying:
All: Take this all of you and eat it; this is my body which will kindle your passion for God and for all God's creatures.

Then Jesus took a cup of wine, praised God, shared the cup saying:
All: Take this all of you and drink from it; this is the cup of my blood, the blood that will energize you with Spirit love; it will be poured out as kindling for the transformation of all.

Let us proclaim the mystery of wonder in our midst: Christ is the spark of love in whom we believe; Christ is the passion of God in whom we trust; Christ will be always the desire who consumes us. As we celebrate this memory of Jesus, let us pray that we, like the disciples on the road to Emmaus, will burn with love for the God of Surprises who breaks the bread of life and pours the cup of salvation over all creation.

Part Four:

May our hearts be merry on our journey as we dream new dreams and see new visions. May we recognize Christ present in every person everywhere: all of us the Body of Christ - broken and shared. Every day as we care for each other, may we encounter the God who dwells with us anew. May we become Spirit-Fire, as we fan the flames of love over the entire cosmos.

Shekinah, be with our families and friends, the young and old, the sick and dying and all those who need your nurturing love this day. Reconcile all those who experience the pain of discrimination in our church. Bless, protect, heal, encourage, comfort each person and group we remember today: (Pause and name people you want to remember.)

As you led the Israelites through the bleak terrain, guide all those who are on their way home to you. (Pause and name people who have died whom you want to remember.)

Open us to Spirit-Fire igniting the Earth. May all creation dance in your presence. May we become one heart, one mind, one spirit with everything. May we touch the earth with reverent awe and live in harmony with all creatures. May we turn away from all efforts to dominate anyone or anything. May we see your face shining in the stars and in the sun. May we embrace the universe's treasures and celebrate life's simple pleasures each day. May your love kindle our friendship with all life. O Heart of Love, we dwell as one in you.

All: Through Christ, with Christ, in Christ the love of God is poured out into the whole world through the power of the Holy Spirit forever and ever. Amen.

The Prayer of Jesus: (Traditional or see appendix)

Breaking of Bread:

(Hold up bread and wine) Let us share the Body of Christ with the Body of Christ! Amen.

Communion:

Sing the "Eight-fold Alleluia" then make up own verses or "Glory to Thee O God of Life" by John Michael Talbot from *The God of Life* or "Veni Sancte Spiritus" from Taize or "You Are the Song" by Miriam Therese Winter from Medical Mission Sisters.

Prayer after Communion:
Thank you for this holy meal that we have shared. Fuel our hearts with your divine energy that we may share your love with all creatures. May we live always as instruments of your faithful love. Amen.

Final Blessing of Community:
May the fire of God's love ignite our hearts in love; may the passion of God radiate through us; may the Spirit of truth and justice burn within us forever. Amen.

Closing Song:
"One by One" by Miriam Therese Winter from Medical Mission Sisters or "We Give Thanks to You, Dear Earth" by Jahn Aldredge-Clanton, published by Twenty-Third 800-321-0411 or "Thanks to Thee" by John Michael Talbot from *The God of Life*.

Liturgy for All Saints' and/or All Souls' Day

Introduction of Theme:
Our departed loved ones are like stars in the night sky, lighting our way to heaven. They belong to a cloud of witnesses, the communion of saints, our saints, who help us on our journey home.

Opening Song:
"For All The Saints" or "God of The Gathering" by Kathy Sherman on cassette *Faces of The Children*" - Sisters of St. Joseph of LaGrange, 1515 W. Ogden Ave., LaGrange, IL 60526-1721

Opening Prayer:
Today we rejoice in the holy women and men of every generation. We remember the saints in our families, among our friends, the saints with whom we identify, the saints we are becoming.

Readings:
1 John 3:1-3 Matthew 5:1-12

Homily:
Reflect on one or more of the following questions.
Who are the saints that you most admire?
What are the modern-day saints?
What does it mean to be a saint today?
Are you and others that you know "saints-in the making"?

Shared Dialogue:
The community shares their thoughts on the theme.

Intercessions:
That we may be Christ-bearers to all in need, especially those who experience rejection, alienation, injustice and poverty, we pray... (Response is: Hear us, O God!)

That we may celebrate the Divine Presence in all whom we encounter, we pray...

That the sick may be healed, especially (mention names), we pray...

That the dead , our beloved family and friends, and all who have gone before us, may dwell forever in God's presence, we pray...
(Other Intentions)

Presentation of Gifts:

(Each community member is invited to write the names of loved ones on a piece of paper to be placed on the altar with the bread and wine, while all present remember our beloved saints in our family, among our friends and neighbors.

Blessed are you, God of all Life. Through your goodness we offer these gifts: bread, wine, our lives and the lives of those we love.

The Eucharistic Prayer:

Part One:

We thank you, our God, that throughout history you have called to the human family and taught us to love one another and to learn, from creation, your compassion and wisdom. May the saintly women and men of old, the cloud of witnesses who have gone before us, accompany us on our journey.

As we wait with joyful hearts for the fulfillment of your plan in our lives, we remember the prophets, martyrs, saints and mystics who have gone before us: Deborah, Judith, Isaiah, Mary of Magdala, Peter, Martha, Paul, Phoebe, Junia, Lydia, Patrick, Brigit of Kildare, Hildegarde of Bingen, Catherine of Siena, Ignatius Loyola, Teresa of Avila, Sojourner Truth, Martin Luther King, Rosa Parks, and all those we remember as heros and heroines in our church who inspire us today.

(Community names, mentors whom they want to remember, living and dead. This list is only partial. Each community shares their own according to custom and culture.)

Part Two:

As we share this holy meal, we remember the holy men and women who drank from Wisdom's well and showed us how to live as courageous disciples: the prophet Miriam, Mary, Mother of Jesus, the woman at the well, Prisca and Aquila, Clare and Francis of Assisi, Dorothy Day, Jean Donovan, Dorothy Kazel, Ita Ford, Maura Clark, Oscar Romero and all those companions we cherish and who bless and challenge us on our faith journey.

All: Holy, holy, holy, God of sinners and of saints, Lover of saints-in-the-making, wisdom of the heavens and of the gentle earth, blessed are all who love in the grace of God!

We honor the ones who have revealed your ways to us until we could recognize them for ourselves. We thank you for the courage and fidelity of all the ones you sent to prepare a path for us to follow - the holy women and men of every age, race and culture.

Part Three:

We especially thank you, Nurturing God, for Jesus, who accompanys us on our journey. Energize us in our work for justice and equality as your holy people. Let your Spirit come upon these gifts to make them holy and fill us with your presence.. May we become the Body of Christ serving the Body of Christ in all that we are and in all that we do.

On the night before Jesus died, he came to table with the women and men he loved. Jesus took bread, blessed and broke the bread and gave it to his friends and said:

All: Take it and eat, this is my body given for you. Do this in memory of me.

At the end of the meal Jesus took a cup of wine, raised it in blessing, gave it to his friends, and said:

All: This is the cup of the new covenant of my blood poured out for you. As often you drink of it, do so in remembrance of me.

Now then, let us proclaim the mystery of our faith:

In every creature that has ever breathed, Christ has lived;

in every living being that has passed on before us, Christ has died; in everything yet to be, Christ will come again!

Part Four:

O Holy One who lives in our hearts, we celebrate your radiant image in men and women everywhere. Your creativity flows through our beings. Your joy fills us. Your blessings are the wellspring of grace all around us. Your mercy is fresh, like dew, every morning. Your healing liberates us from all darkness and oppression. Your empowerment bubbles up inside us. For you are the Love that dwells in our depths, the Wisdom of the Ages that speaks within us and through us, You are the Divine Passion that makes us all one. Amen.

All: Through Christ, with Christ, in Christ the love of God is poured out to all through the power of the Holy Spirit forever and ever. Amen.

The Prayer of Jesus: (Traditional Our Father, Our Mother)

Breaking of Bread:
(Hold up bread and wine) Let us share the Body of Christ with the Body of Christ! Happy are we and all who have gone before us to become part of the Communion of Saints
All: Jesus you make us worthy to receive you and become you for others. We are the Body of Christ.

Communion:
"United as One" by Owen Alstoff, or "Pan De Vida" by Bob Hurd,or "Seek Ye First" by Karen Lafferty

Prayer after Communion:
Holy One, we praise your glory reflected in our saints. May we who share at this table be filled with your love and celebrate with joyful hearts our communion with all the saints. Amen.

Final Blessing of Community:
May the God of Sarah and Abraham bless us; may the God of Jesus and Mary Magdalene bless us; may the God of our mothers and our fathers bless us and may we always celebrate our oneness in the communion of the saints.

Closing Song:
"When the Saints Go Marching In"

Liturgy to Celebrate Justice, Partnership and Equality for Women in Church and Society

Gathering Song and Greeting:
Presider: In the name of God, our mother and father, and of Jesus our brother and healer, and of the Holy Spirit, our wisdom and guide.
ALL: Amen.
Presider: May God, the Blessed Holy Three, be with us as we work together for partnership, justice and equality for women in church and society!
ALL: And also with you.

Penitential Rite:
Presider: O God, may we see your feminine face in our female ancestors and in all women. **ALL:** May we open our hearts, like Mary, to God's mothering love.
Presider: Jesus the Christ, may we see the divine reality in the person of a woman especially in women who have been abused and exploited.
ALL: May we like Mary, champion the oppressed and stand with our sisters who are abused and exploited.
Presider: O Wisdom/Sophia, may we see you in men and women who have been caring partners and companions **ALL:** May we, like Mary, live a connectedness and friendship with others.
Presider: May the God of love, forgive us our lack of trust in your Spirit Sophia moving with us, in us, and through us, leading us to guidance, courage, healing and empowerment.
ALL: Amen.
ALL: Glory to God in the highest, and peace, justice and equality to God's people on earth. O loving God, in the name of the Holy Three-in-One we worship you, we give you thanks, we praise you for your glory. O Jesus Christ, holy Child of our God, You who liberate and heal us: have mercy on us. You, who are all Goodness and Light, hold us in your heart forever. For you are the Holy One; you are our liberator our healer, our strength, O Blessed Holy Three: Jesus Christ; with the Holy Spirit, in the glory of God. Amen.

Liturgy of the Word

First Reading:
Isaiah 58:5-8 "Loose the bonds of injustice."

Responsorial Psalm:
Psalm 6:2 "O God heal me for my bones are shaking with terror."

Second Reading:
John 13:34-35 "Love one another."
Gospel Acclamation: ALLELUIA! (sung)
Reader: A reading from the Gospel according to Luke 1:39-56 (Magnificat)
"For God has done great things for me."
ALL: Glory to you O God.
Reader: The good news of Jesus, the Christ!
ALL: Glory and praise to you, Jesus, the Christ!

Homily:
Profession of Faith:
ALL: We believe in God who is creator and nurturer of all. We believe in Jesus, the Christ, who is our love, our hope, and our light. We believe in the Holy Spirit, the breath of Wisdom Sophia , who energizes and guides us to build caring communities and to challenge oppression, exploitation and injustices. We believe that God loves us passionately and forgives us everything. We believe that we are radiant images of God who calls us to live fully, love tenderly, and serve generously. We believe in the communion of saints our heavenly friends, who support us on life's journey. We believe in the partnership and equality of women and men in our church and world. We believe that all are one in the Heart of God. We believe that women's liberation is human liberation. Here we dwell in loving relationships. Here we live our prophetic call of Gospel equality.

General Intercessions:
Presider: Aware that God, like a fierce mother bear who protects her young, is a defender of the oppressed and pursuer of justice, we now bring the women in our lives, in our church and world, before

you . We pray for healing, justice and empowerment, partnership and equality.

(After each intercession, the response is: Loving God, hear our prayer.)

For mothers and grandmothers, we pray for healing

For daughters and granddaughters, we pray for empowerment

For a global sisterhood in which women support other women, we pray for guidance

For women who have been abused, we pray for empowerment.

For women who have confronted their abusers, we pray for courage

For young girls who have been sexually exploited, we pray for healing.

For the support of women friends, we pray for your blessing.

For the men and women who have been caring friends and partners, we pray for their continued growth and well being.

Presider: In your name we pray that we can do all things by the power of your Spirit working in us. All: Amen

Preparation of the Gifts:

Presider: Blessed are you, O God, Creator of all. Through your divine providence we have this bread to offer, which earth has given and human hands have made, it will become for us the Bread of Life.

ALL: Blessed be God forever.

Presider: Blessed are you, O God, Creator of all. Through your divine providence we have this wine to offer, fruit from our vines tended by human toil, it will become our spiritual drink.

ALL: Blessed be God forever.

Presider: Nurturing God, we are united in this sacrament by the love of Jesus Christ in communion with Mary, who proclaimed God's power and mercy for the lowly and oppressed. Like Mary, First Disciple, may we speak out when women suffer neglect and abuse . May we live as prophetic witnesses that women's rights are human rights. Like Mary, may we discover the liberating power of Woman-Spirit in our midst. We ask this through Wisdom Sophia, Jesus, our brother, and the Holy Spirit.

ALL: Amen.

Presider: God dwells in you and in all women.

ALL: And also with you.

Presider: Lift up your hearts and pursue justice.

ALL: We lift them up to God, Pursuer of Justice.

Presider: Let us give thanks to the Creator of all.

ALL: It is right to give God thanks and praise.

Eucharistic Prayer:
Presider: O loving God, O blessed Holy Three, who brings to birth the world of our dreams for mutual respect and partnership, we do well always and everywhere to give you praise. Give us courage to act justly and work collaboratively to change systems that keep women poor and marginalized in our society. We thank you for the women and men who are working for justice and equality in our church and world. Each day you embrace us in a circle of love; your spirit dwelling in us immerses us in the depths of your presence in the cosmos and gives us the hope of everlasting joy with you. Your gift of the Spirit, who raised Jesus from the dead, gives us hope that one day all will be one at the eternal banquet of heaven. With thankful hearts in the company of the angels and saints, we praise you, God of Abundance and Welcome.
ALL: Holy, Holy, Holy God, God of strength and light. Heaven and earth are full of Your glory.
Hosanna in the highest. Blessed are all who come in the name of our God. Hosanna in the highest.
Presider: You are holy indeed O nurturing God. You are the Heart of Love. You affirm women's bodies as holy and women's stories as sacred. Pour out your Spirit upon all who work for justice and equality for women in church and society. Pour out your spirit upon this bread and wine so that with these gifts we may become the body and blood of Jesus, the Christ, in whom we have all become your daughters and sons. On the night before he died, Jesus came to table with the women and men he loved. Jesus took bread and praised you, God of compassion. He blessed and broke the bread, gave it to his friends and said:
All: "Take, eat, this is my body, given for you. Do this in remembrance of me.
Presider: After supper, Jesus poured the final cup of wine and blessed you, God of the Cosmos. Jesus shared the cup with his friends, and said:
All: This is the cup of the covenant of my love poured out for you. As often as you drink of it, remember me.
Presider: Let us proclaim the mystery of faith:

ALL: Christ, our love, has died in every woman who has been beaten, Christ, our hope, is risen in all who work for justice and equality, Christ, our life, will come again in a new Pentecost.

Presider: In memory of Jesus, who showed us the path to liberation and empowerment, we offer you, Loving Creator, the bread of life, this saving cup. We give thanks for the loving relationships that helped us grow more aware of our goodness, strength, and passion. We give thanks that we live in your Enfolding Presence and serve you with grateful hearts. May we be advocates for survivors of violence, abuse, and rape. May we accompany them on their journey to empowerment, forgiveness, and wholeness. May all of us who share in this sacred banquet of Christ be brought together as one in the Holy Spirit and be filled with courage to live Gospel equality in inclusive communities working for justice and peace in our church and world.

God, remember your holy people throughout the world, make us one in love, together with Benedict our pope, _____, our bishop(s), and all God's people.

Remember our brothers and sisters who are homeless, hungry, sick, lonely, in prison. Remember our sisters and brothers, who face oppression, discrimination and joblessness, who have lost homes, partners, and hope.

Remember all those who work for justice and who have given their lives for the needs of people who suffer injustice especially Maura Clark, Ita Ford, Jean Donovan, Dorothy Kazel, Irene McCormack, and Bishop Oscar Romero, who have gone to their rest in the hope of rising again, _____(pause and invite community to name others) bring them and all the departed into your everlasting arms.

Have mercy on us all; make us one with Mary, Mother of Jesus, our sister and, champion of the oppressed and the apostles through the ages, especially Mary of Magdala, Junia and Andronicus, Dorothy Day, Martin Luther King, Rosa Parks, Sojourner Truth, Josephine Bakhita and all the holy women and men who have done your will throughout the ages. May their courage inspire us to confront patriarchal systems that discriminate against women. God, let it be so as we we praise you in union with he holy women and men of every generation who are free at last from all bondage and injustice, and give you glory through Jesus the Christ.

ALL: Through Christ, With Christ and In Christ, in the unity of the Holy Spirit, may our work for justice, peace and equality give You glory and honor, Holy God forever and ever. AMEN.

The Prayer of Jesus:

ALL: Our Father and Mother…

Presider: Protect us, God, from all evil and dismiss all anxiety from our minds. May a thousand angels guide our steps to live justice, partnership and equality now as we wait in joyful hope for the coming of God in our time where all can say, "thank God, we are free at last!"

ALL: For the kindom, the power, and the glory are yours, now and forever. Amen.

The Sign of Peace:

Presider: Jesus, the Christ, You said to your disciples, "My peace I leave you. My peace I give you." May the love of God fill us with peace. May the healing power of Christ strengthen us. May the Holy Spirit empower us.

ALL: Amen.

Presider: May the peace of God be always with you.

ALL: And also with you.

Presider: Let us offer each other a sign of peace.

Litany for the Breaking of the Bread:

ALL: Loving God, You call us to speak truth to power, have mercy on us. Loving God, You call us to live the Gospel of peace and justice, have mercy on us. Loving God, You call us to be Your presence in the world. Grant us peace.

Presider: This is Jesus, who called women and men to be partners and equals, and who liberates, heals and transforms us and our world. All are invited to partake of this sacred banquet of love.

ALL: Jesus you make us worthy to receive you and become you for others. We are the Body of Christ.

Prayer After Communion:
Presider:
The encompassing of God be on us,
The encompassing of the God of healing,
The encompassing of Christ be on us,
The encompassing of the Christ of love,
The encompassing of the Spirit be on us,
The encompassing of the Spirit of Grace,
Let us go forth from this Banquet of love, aware always that human rights are equal rights and that we are all the beloved of God.
(Adapted from Alexander Carmichael's *Carmina Gadelica*)
ALL: Amen.

Concluding Rite:
Presider: Our God is with you
ALL: and also with you.

Blessing:
(everyone please extend your hands in mutual blessing)
ALL: May the fire of God's love warm your hearts.
May God grant your prayers for justice for women in our church and world.
May the love of Christ work though you to lighten the load of inequality and injustice that our sisters carry.
May the wind be always at your back.
May the sun shine warm upon your face.
And the rain fall soft upon your fields.
And until we meet again,
May you be held in the palm of God's hands.
(Old Irish Blessing)

Dismissal:
Presider: Go in the peace of Christ. Let the service for justice and equality continue!
ALL: Thanks be to God.

Concluding Hymn

Alternative and Contemporary Versions of the Prayer of Jesus:
O Passionate God of Love, You dwell in the hearts of all people.
Intimate Warmth is your Name. May your tenderness be felt.
Embrace us this day in your compassionate arms.
Forgive us our failures to love and heal the hurts of our hearts
And give us the power to heal one another.
Help us to let go of resentment and all that separates us from one another.
Deliver us from hostility.
For Yours is the brilliant beauty and maginificent power of Divine Love forever. Amen.

Our Birther God who dwells among us, we praise your holy name.
Your love be born in us. Your will be done. You give us all we need.
You forgive us and help us to forgive others.
You deliver us from evil and liberate us to live in freedom.
For you are the Creator, the Lover and the Empowerer that enfolds us forever
In your Divine Womb-Love. Amen.

O God of Love, You dwell everywhere.
Holy is your passionate presence everywhere and in everyone.
Your vision be praised; Your dreams be fulfilled in us and in all generations.
You give us all we need to be free and whole.
You forgive us our failures and heal the wounds of our souls.
For yours is the power and glory that dwells everywhere in the cosmos, forever and ever. Amen.

About the Author:

Dr. Bridget Mary Meehan, RCWP, is the author of eighteen books including *The Healing Power of Prayer, Praying with Women of the Bible,* and *Praying with Visionary Women.* She is the dean of the Doctor of Ministry program for Global Ministries University. On July 31, 2006, Bridget Mary Meehan was ordained a Roman Catholic priest, one of the first twelve women in the United States, and a bishop on April 19, 2009. Bridget Mary serves as a spiritual leader of the Association of Roman Catholic Women Priests and presides at liturgies with Mary, Mother of Jesus Inclusive Catholic Community, in Sarasota, Florida and in Falls Church, Virginia.

For more information, visit:
www.associationofromancatholicwomenpriests.org
http://www.marymotherofjesus.org
Bridget Mary's Blog: http://bridgetmarys.blogspot.com/